FREEDOM AND REACTANCE

COMPLEX HUMAN BEHAVIOR

A series of volumes edited by
Leon Festinger and Stanley Schachter

FREEDOM AND REACTANCE

BY ROBERT A. WICKLUND

UNIVERSITY OF TEXAS AT AUSTIN

 LAWRENCE ERLBAUM ASSOCIATES, PUBLISHERS
1974   Potomac, Maryland

DISTRIBUTED BY THE HALSTED PRESS DIVISION OF

JOHN WILEY & SONS
New York   Toronto   London   Sydney

Lawrence Erlbaum Associates, Publishers
12736 Lincolnshire Drive
Potomac, Maryland 20854

Distributed solely by Halsted Press Division
John Wiley & Sons, Inc., New York

Library of Congress Cataloging in Publication Data

Wicklund, Robert A.
    Freedom and reactance.

    (Complex human behavior)
    Includes bibliographical references.
    1. Free will and determinism. I. Title.
BF620.W5   155.9'2   74-4004
ISBN 0-470-94255-X

Printed in the United States of America

CONTENTS

PREFACE

Brehm's theory of psychological reactance has marked the beginning of a psychological investigation into the consequences of losing freedom. The concept "freedom" has been touched upon intermittently by disciplines such as political science and philosophy, and even on occasion by psychology, but Brehm's treatment has been the first analysis of freedom to spark experimental investigations into the variety of reactions to infringements on freedom. This book has been written to capture the many directions taken by the theory since 1966, and to integrate reactance theory with theoretical ideas that apply to some of the same phenomena.

Psychological reactance is the motivational state of the person whose freedom has been assaulted. The child who does the opposite of his parents' instructions is acting out of reactance, and so is the person who comes to love Shakespeare merely because the tickets to the play are sold out. The child is reacting against attempted influence, whereas the newcomer to Shakespeare is reacting against the impossibility of gaining entrance to the play. These two instances are the basic points of application of the theory, and since the theory's inception these two themes have been expanded in several directions.

Within the experimental laboratory reactance has been expanded to political and social problems. Several studies have found the conditions for obtaining boomerang effects due to high-pressure influence attempts, including censorship of potentially persuasive material. Numerous studies imply that a forceful, domineering, or one-sided communicator is often likely to meet with failure due to the freedom-threatening nature of his style of presentation. Attraction to hard-to-get members of the opposite sex, refusal to help others in need, and reactions to infringements on personal territory all fall within the boundaries of reactance processes. Finally, on the level of the individual, questions have been asked about the conditions leading a person to like things he cannot have. Experiments show that a time delay, physical effort, or monetary infringement will increase a person's attraction to that for which he must wait, suffer, or pay.

Aside from the diverse areas of application, what has happened to the theory itself? Throughout the chapters information from experiments and theoretical speculation are put together to assess the accuracy of the original theory, ask questions about new areas of application, and raise issues not yet resolved. One of the more imposing theoretical issues is raised under the heading of self-imposed threats to freedom. Oddly enough, self-imposed infringements on freedom seem to be a formidable source of reactance.

A great debt I happily acknowledge to Charles R. Ervin, Russell A. Jones, Judson Mills, Melvin L. Snyder, and Stephen Worchel for their insightful readings of several chapters. To Jack W. Brehm I owe a particular gratitude for a detailed and critical reading of the entire manuscript, coupled with frequent encouragement. Finally, Claudia A. Cates merits special mention for her occasional cogent criticisms and for her accurate typing of two versions of the manuscript.

R.A.W.

March, 1974

ACKNOWLEDGEMENTS

A number of sources have very kindly granted permission to use material previously published elsewhere. Thanks and acknowledgement are due to the following:

Academic Press, Inc., for permission to reprint material used in the following figures and tables:

Figure 4 from Wicklund, Slattum, & Solomon, *Journal of Experimental Social Psychology*. Copyright 1970 by Academic Press, Inc. Reprinted by permission.

Table 2 from Brehm, *A theory of psychological reactance*. Copyright 1966 by Academic Press, Inc. Reprinted by permission.

Table 5 from Worchel & Arnold, *Journal of Experimental Social Psychology*. Copyright 1973 by Academic Press, Inc. Reprinted by permission.

Table 7 from Jones & Brehm, *Journal of Experimental Social Psychology*. Copyright 1970 by Academic Press, Inc. Reprinted by permission.

Table 8 from Wicklund & Brehm, *Journal of Experimental Social Psychology*. Copyright 1968 by Academic Press, Inc. Reprinted by permission.

Table 9 from Brehm, *A theory of psychological reactance*. Copyright 1966 by Academic Press, Inc. Reprinted by permission.

Table 18 from Knott, Nunnally, & Duchnowski, *Journal of Experimental Research in Personality*. Copyright 1967 by Academic Press, Inc. Reprinted by permission.

Table 21 from Brehm, Stires, Sensenig & Shaban, *Journal of Experimental Social Psychology*. Copyright 1966 by Academic Press, Inc. Reprinted by permission.

Table 30 from Brehm, *A theory of psychological reactance*. Copyright 1966 by Academic Press, Inc. Reprinted by permission.

The American Psychological Association, for permission to reprint material used in the following tables:

Table 1 from Heller, Pallak, & Picek, *Journal of Personality and Social Psychology*. Copyright 1973 by The American Psychological Association. Reprinted by permission.

Table 6 from Jones, *Journal of Personality and Social Psychology*. Copyright 1970 by The American Psychological Association. Reprinted by permission.

Tables 10 and 11 from Worchel & Brehm, *Journal of Personality and Social Psychology*. Copyright 1970 by The American Psychological Association. Reprinted by permission.

Table 12 from Sensenig & Brehm, *Journal of Personality and Social Psychology*. Copyright 1968 by The American Psychological Association. Reprinted by permission.

Tables 13 and 14 Worchel & Brehm, *Journal of Personality and Social Psychology*. Copyright 1971 by The American Psychological Association. Reprinted by permission.

FREEDOM AND REACTANCE

1
INTRODUCTION TO REACTANCE THEORY AND AN OUTLINE OF TOPICS

INTRODUCTION TO "FREEDOM"

This is a book about freedom and the psychological consequences of *1st assumption* taking freedom away. The point of view adopted here assumes that humans often believe and act as if they are their own masters—that they can control and master their own fate. Whether or not people do in fact control their own destinies is not an immediate issue. The only important assumption is that each of us believes largely in a free-will doctrine regarding our own behaviors. On a more molecular level, what does it mean for a person to think he is free?

A person is free only by virtue of his decisions. If someone has several possibilities set before him but cannot of his own power bring some of these possibilities into play for himself, the concept of freedom is then irrelevant. Otherwise stated, he is unfree. The very nature of freedom implies the person's potential to alter his present situation, meaning that he may decide not to change it, or to alter it in any of several directions. A religious man may see two possibilities for his afterlife: heaven or hell. Given his religious background he believes that he can affect the status of his afterlife through his worldly actions, thus he is free with respect to these two alternatives in that he may decide which of them to pursue during his life. (Whether or not the rest of us think he is free to pursue either heaven or hell is not an issue.) The same man may also believe strongly that humans are of such a nature that war is a perpetual inevitability. Again, there are two possible states he might experience, war or peace, but the difference between this and the first example hinges on the potential in the situation for a decision. If he is convinced that none of his actions could affect the course of the war-and-peace cycle, then he simply has no freedom with regard to these two alternatives.

In this conception of free behaviors there is no assumption that the decision is an overt commitment, an unequivocal act, or even publicly ob-

1

decision servable. "Decision" is defined broadly: A person has the power of decision if he believes he can alter his present situation.

Perhaps a comment about the definition of "behavior" is appropriate in specifying the nature of free behavior. Free behaviors are not just molar instrumental actions. Also included are emotions, attitudes, and any other feeling states of the organism, provided that the organism feels the power to alter these feeling states as he sees fit. People can easily have freedom in regard to feelings of pity, contempt, and similar states, and people regularly exercise their freedom to adopt various stands on opinion issues.

Given the central assumption that individuals believe they can significantly control their own destinies, or at least that they can control many specific behaviors, it becomes possible to examine the effects of infringements on these free behaviors. Accordingly, the second central assumption of this book *2nd assumption* is this: When a freedom is infringed upon, the person will react in such a way as to reassert and protect that freedom. The second assumption will receive some elaboration in several examples to be presented shortly, but first, the perspective of the pages to follow can now be introduced.

The two assumptions stated above are the basic elements of a theory of psychological reactance proposed by Brehm (1966). The remainder of this chapter is a characterization of the various kinds of freedoms that are the focus of the theory and its associated research, a description of the theory in some detail, and an introduction of several explanatory ideas that may parallel or contradict the theory. This chapter might be viewed as a model of the entire book, for the major themes throughout the book consist of research on threatened freedom, interpretations offered by reactance theory, and points of similarity between the theory and other conceptions.

In order to give the reader an appreciation of the kinds of freedoms dealt with in research on freedom, three examples are provided below. Each of these three represents a major topic area of the book—the topic areas being the following: (*a*) social influence, (*b*) barriers, and (*c*) self-imposed threats to freedom. The book is divided into these three sections because of the existence of three generically different types of threat to freedom. Discussion of the theory and related research is greatly facilitated by this tripartite division, because each of the three types of threats requires its own theoretical assumptions and because the kinds of situations used to create reactance differ considerably among the three divisions.

Reactance theory stipulates several variables that determine the amount of reactance aroused by a threat to freedom, and these variables are examined within each of the three sections of the book. There is an attempt to create a parallel between the three sections with respect to the theoretical variables, in order to facilitate understanding of a particular variable across all three divisions. For example, one of the central variables is the importance of a threatened freedom. The operation of that variable will be examined first in the social influence section, then in the section on barriers, and finally within the self-imposed threat section. In this way it will be possible to assess whether or not the importance-of-freedom variable operates the same way for each of the three generic sources of threat to freedom.

The following three examples typify the threats to freedom found within each of the three topic areas. After the examples are presented the elements of the theory will be summarized in detail.

Social Influence

A 14-year-old boy holds the opinion that the driving age in his state should be lowered from 16 to 14. He is eager to learn to drive, is familiar with numerous arguments and studies relevant to the issue, and sees no reason for keeping the minimum age at the "absurd level of 16 years old." One day he learns that the head of the state patrol has been invited to his school to give a talk favorable to lowering the present driving age, and of course the boy gleefully anticipates this talk. Shortly before the talk is to begin, there is a school-wide announcement that the talk has been canceled by the school superintendent on the grounds that teenagers should not hear an appeal for a lowered driving age. Immediately after the cancellation the boy's driving-age attitude becomes more adamant than ever. He adopts an extreme and radical position in favor of lowering the minimum age to 12 years old.

The free behavior in this case consists of the boy's attitude. He is familiar with the issue, capable of responding to new facts about the issue, and should feel that his attitude is the product of his own thinking and gathering of information. He is free to adopt whatever attitude he feels is most correct. Now a censorship takes place, such that the boy perceives an attempt at mind control. From the boy's standpoint the superintendent intends to keep the minds of schoolchildren away from thoughts of liberalized driving ages. There is no apparent attempt to convey information, but simply an obvious attempt to influence opinion.

How does reactance theory conceptualize this attempt at influence? When a person feels free to hold any attitude on an issue, that freedom becomes threatened whenever he feels pressure to change his attitude. Depending upon the source of influence and other factors to be introduced in later chapters, the pressure may be more or less effective in threatening freedom, but the important principle is this: Whenever someone finds that another tries to influence his attitude, the freedom to hold any possible position on the attitude will be threatened.

Tentatively granting that freedom of attitudes can be threatened by intended influence, what happens next? "Psychological reactance," abbreviated "reactance," is set up whenever a freedom encounters interference, i.e., whenever the freedom is threatened with elimination or actually eliminated. Reactance is a motivational state with the property of keeping the person's freedoms safeguarded. It is a motivational state working in opposition to forces that interfere with freedoms, and it comes into play to the extent that any freedom is threatened with impairment. In the case of threats to freedom of attitudes, the effects of reactance are easy to describe, for they operate as simple counterforces. The more a person feels pushed in a given direction, the more reactance will move him in the opposite direction. This principle was illustrated in the example by the "boomerang effect" of the influence attempt. Instead of causing the boy to comply with a more conservative stand on the issue, the censorship resulted in just the opposite. In young children this is known as negativity.

What is the function of reactance? In the instance of the example, what purpose is served by the boy's negativistic or boomerang reaction? Certainly his parents or other bystanders might describe the reaction as silly, irrational, and unnecessary. The function of reactance is this. Since reactance is a motivational state directed toward preservation of freedom, it will lead the individual in the direction of exercising the threatened freedom. By exercising the freedom, the boy can demonstrate to himself that he still has the freedom, and that the freedom has not been conquered or otherwise diminished.

Without the operation of reactance forces the boy would have been influenced in the direction dictated by the superintendent censor. There would have been no forces to hold him back from following the pressures to be influenced, and were the boy to examine himself after succumbing to the influence, he would find that his freedom was neither strong nor viable.

Why can't reactance lead the person not to react at all? That is, why didn't the boy freeze in his pre-existing attitude when confronted by the pressure to change? Was a negativistic response necessary? The answer is quite simple. Being free means that a person can go in any of several directions (we will limit this to two directions for the present discussion), and a threat to freedom will inevitably force the individual toward one of those potential directions. But the motivational state of reactance is also directional. It impels the person to reassert the freedom, and because of this directionality the individual does not "sit still" when freedom is threatened. The rational observer, musing over the young man whose freedom has just been threatened, might think the rational response to censorship would be to maintain the original attitude—to show zero change. But the forces of reactance do not allow for this. There will always be forces moving the person in a direction opposite the one implied by the threat.

As will be seen in some detail in later chapters, there are other theoretical analyses of effects such as that illustrated by the case of the young man and the censored speech. One of the more persuasive of these is known as balance

pared c̄
balance theory

theory. As applied to persuasive communications, the balance notion operates as follows.

The young man undoubtedly perceived a close tie between the superintendent and the conservative point of view. Therefore, whether or not the young man accepts that point of view will be dependent on his relationship to the superintendent. If he has a fondness for the superintendent, the cognitive balance principle would hold that the young man will also be fond of those things closely and positively associated with the superintendent, including a conservative view of the driving-age issue. On the other hand, if the young gentleman has no use for the superintendent, the balance principle would dictate that the conservative viewpoint and other aspects of the superintendent would be rejected. Stated in other terms, the balance notion indicates that cognitive balance is achieved when we dissociate ourselves from those things positively associated with people we dislike; and likewise, cognitive balance is achieved when we associate ourselves with those things positively associated with people we like.

In the case of censorship it is entirely plausible that the superintendent's behavior insulted, frustrated, and affronted the young man and his peers. In short, the censor's actions perhaps resulted in his being actively disliked among the students. It would follow from the balance principle that they would dissociate themselves from his opinions, and this obviously implies the obtained effect, which was a more extreme attitude in the direction away from the censor's position.

This is a case in which reactance theory and balance theory each offer reasonable interpretations of the boomerang effect. Does this mean that the selection of reactance theory rather than balance theory as the focus of this book is arbitrary? As will be made explicit in later chapters, the reason for focusing on reactance theory is its wealth of associated variables. There are numerous variables within the theory indicating the precise conditions under which reactance can be aroused, and by implementing such variables the theory's predictive power gains, as well as the researcher's ability to disentangle reactance processes from balance processes and other theoretical mechanisms.

One such variable is "importance of freedom." Brehm (1966) defines importance as ". . . the unique instrumental value which [a] behavior has for (*?*) the satisfaction of needs, multiplied by the actual or potential maximum magnitude of those needs [pp. 4–5]." A set of alternative behaviors would be important if those behaviors were alternative routes to saving one's own life. In such a case the freedom to select the most suitable possible route would be of maximal importance. By way of contrast, a totally unimportant freedom would be a nondrinker's freedom to select any of 30 brands of bourbon. The freedom has no bearing on need satisfaction, thus the freedom is trivial. How is the importance concept extended to attitudes? If a set of possible attitudes deals with central behaviors, such as a person's alternative routes to saving his own life, we would think that the freedom to hold any of the several possible attitudes toward those behaviors would be of high importance. But if the attitudes have to do with liquor and the person possessing this freedom of attitude is a teetotaler, the freedom to adopt any attitude is of no consequence. In summary, if a set of attitudes deals with central and necessary behaviors, the freedom of attitude is of high importance.

Back to the driving-age issue. If we compare the young man in question with one of his contemporaries who never intends to drive, there is an obvious difference in the importance of the freedom to adopt any position. Both 14-year olds have the freedom of attitude, but the freedom is much more important for the boy who wants to drive. Reactance theory stipulates that reactance will be aroused only to the degree that a freedom is important, and if the two young men were compared, only the would-be driver would show a boomerang effect. This is the reactance theory prediction. But balance theory would offer approximately the same prediction for each boy, for each of them should be negatively impressed by the censor, and both should dissociate themselves from the censor's apparent position.

It should be apparent that the introduction of the importance-of-freedom variable allows a distinction between the application of the two theories. If the two boys react differentially to the censorship, it becomes clear that the specificity of reactance theory gives it some advantage over the balance notion, for balance theory does not explicitly take into account the importance of the attitudes in question.

Other variables within reactance theory could also be brought to bear on the balance vs. reactance question of interpretation, but these will be introduced in the following examples. It might be added that other theoretical approaches to the boomerang effect could be discussed, but they will be reserved for later chapters. The major purpose of introducing balance theory at this stage is simply to offer some appreciation of the connection between reactance theory and its alternatives, and to illustrate one way to discriminate among the possible explanations of the boomerang effect.

Barriers

A boy who has shown interest in girls for several years has a list of girls he asks out from time to time. He alternates among them, depending on his mood and the social occasion. One evening he phones one of his favorites and asks her to attend a drive-in movie with him the following Saturday. She declines, indicating that her social calendar is full for the next several weeks. Disregarding his various reactions to this disappointment, there is one notable effect soon after his phone call: He becomes increasingly attracted to the girl.

The freedom in this case obviously consists of the several available girls, and the refusal to date him constituted the violation of freedom. Reactance should motivate him to reassert the usurped free behavior, which means that he should try even harder to date her. According to reactance theory there will be an additional effect. Not only will he engage in overt attempts to exercise the restricted behavior of dating the girl in question, but she should also become more attractive from his perspective. Such increased attractiveness is a manifestation of the reassertion of freedom.

A word about barriers is in order. The barrier concept can be defined through the assumption that the organism seeks reward, tries to reduce its drives, and also avoids expenditure of effort. Any event imposing itself between the person and a free behavior (i.e., one of several behaviors that could be chosen) is a barrier, provided that it brings about a reduction in reward and/or an increase in effort. The barrier does not have to be physical. It can be represented symbolically, with the assumption that a symbol has an understandable physical referent.

In the case of the hard-to-get girl the barrier was purely physical, in the sense that the girl was totally unavailable at the time he desired. But other kinds of barriers might have been imposed. For example, she could have been too expensive (demanded an expensive evening on the town rather than a cheap drive-in movie), she may have complied but insisted on a delay of several days, or she might have given him the date on the condition that he exert certain extra efforts.

What is the difference between barriers and intended influence as generic classes of reactance-arousers? First, it should be obvious that social-influence attempts must originate in other people, while barriers can be either social or asocial. Second, and more useful as a generic distinction, barriers have been defined as events that deter reward and/or increase effort expenditure, while social influence does not obviously have this quality. The pressures toward compliance set up by influence attempts are not necessarily related in any strict form to probability of reward or effort to be exerted.

An alternative theoretical approach to barriers and the concept of freedom. When a girl is hard-to-get, the boy chasing her might well assume that she has some particularly attractive qualities rendering her desirable to all males. If so, reactance is unnecessary as a psychological mechanism for interpreting the previous example. We need only assume the boy discovered something about the girl by way of her announcement that she was dated up for several weeks. He discovered a previously unknown popularity and concluded that she must be especially sexy or otherwise desirable.

A straightforward method of disentangling such explanations from the reactance interpretation is to compare a free situation with an unfree situation. Imagine that the boy had called the identical girl, but rather than having chosen her freely, a friend had suggested her as a blind date, and further, the boy had no other prospects in mind. Under these circumstances the girl's refusal should not have aroused reactance, since he had no freedom of choice. However, the alternative explanation proposed should operate independent of whether or not he is free. That is, the observation that the girl already has dates and the conclusion that she therefore must be especially attractive should in no way depend on pre-existing freedom. Accordingly, the increase in attractiveness should be identical in the free and unfree situations if reactance is not a relevant process. But if reactance in response to a violated freedom is at least partially responsible for the increased attractiveness, the girl will appear more attractive following her refusal to the degree that her refusal interfered with the boy's freedom.

The Decision Process

A young woman has two lovers, is strongly attracted to each of them, and has a strong desire to be married (to someone) in the near future. In fact, if she does not marry within a year she will no longer be heir to her father's fortune. She has known each of them so long that it is virtually impossible to learn anything new about either one, but even in the absence of new information about them a curious phenomenon develops regarding her preferences. As the point at which she must marry comes closer, she becomes increasingly conflicted about which man she prefers. A year prior to her estimated time of marriage she sees one as somewhat superior to the other, six months later this differential preference has begun to dissipate, and within a few weeks of her planned decision point she rates them almost equally.

The freedom in this case is a freedom of choice between two distinct overt behaviors, just as in the previous example. Had an outside source of influence attempted to push the young woman toward one of her suitors, reactance should have led her to prefer the opposite. But in this example the curious phenomenon of a gradual convergence in the attractiveness of the two men took place independently of outside pressures. This being the case, what does the example have to do with reactance?

As the woman approaches the decision point she anticipates marrying one man and rejecting the other, a fairly irrevocable decision. The fact of her losing one alternative is an explicit case of a diminished freedom. Reactance should be aroused by this loss, and she will be motivated to restore the freedom. Note that by deciding she restricts her own freedom—there is no outside force stealing one of the men away. Such a self-imposed loss of freedom operates just the same as an externally-imposed loss. No matter whether she or someone else is responsible for eliminating the freedom, reactance will be created. Of course, in the example the woman did not actually decide between the two men—she merely held preferences. The example did not carry her up through the choice point, and the freedom had not yet been eliminated. However, reactance was created anyway, and the process is as follows.

It has been assumed by Linder and Crane (1970), Linder, Wortman, and Brehm (1971), and Wicklund (1968) that a preference carries implications for eventual choice. To the degree that a person has singled out an alternative as preferred, that preference implies to him the eventual selection of that alternative and rejection of others. This means that the preference amounts to a threat to freedom. The preference is an indication, or signal, that a freedom will soon be lost in a particular manner, and as is the case with other threats to freedom, reactance will be generated. As always, reactance results in the reassertion of the threatened freedom. Since the threat in the example took the form of the less preferred alternative being threatened with eventual loss, reactance would lead to the reassertion of the freedom to select that alternative. This means that she will be motivated to bring the lower-rated alternative into strong contention as a choice object. In terms of her preferences for the two men the distance between them will be close, with the originally less-preferred moving up toward equality with the originally preferred. This is known as "predecisional convergence."

One more variable must be accounted for to make complete sense of the example. The convergence phenomenon increased the closer the woman came to her decision point. In order to account for this effect an assumption has been made by the authors just mentioned—an assumption that appears obvious after some examination: The closer the person is to the decision point (or action point), the greater power a preference has to threaten decision freedom. There is a good reason for this assumption. The preference has no implications for action when the decision point is viewed as an abstraction far into the future. A five-year-old boy can indicate a strong preference for driving a garbage truck, or a girl of the same age can indicate a strong attraction to a male friend, and in neither case is there much direct implication for loss of freedom. The decision to be made, whether concerning occupation or mate, is so far off for a five-year old that the connection between a preference and the ultimate decision is nonexistent. But as the decision comes into view and is only weeks or hours off, the statement of preference has a stronger psychological connection with behavior, hence the strong threat value. In short, the woman's increasing tendency to see the alternative men as equally attractive was the result of her preference having an increasingly stronger connection with the forthcoming decision, which means an accelerating threat value. The more the lower-rated man is threatened with loss, the stronger her motivation to bring him into serious consideration as an object of choice.

An alternative conception of the psychological events associated with decision-making has been advanced by Mills (1965, 1968) in the form of a "theory of choice certainty." Reduced to its simplest form, the choice-certainty idea argues that individuals will act so as to convince themselves that they are making wise choices. This means that prior to decisions people will selectively expose themselves to information in order to convince themselves that the to-be-chosen course of action is indeed superior. There is another strategy people will adopt when such information is not accessible. Mills suggests that people will attempt to see the to-be-chosen alternative as better, simply by raising their evaluations of it, and that such a process is especially likely to occur when the decision is close at hand.

It is apparent that the second method of attaining certainty about one's choice, the process of biasing the ratings of alternatives in order that the choice seems clear, implies an effect just the opposite of that described in the example. According to Mills, the young woman would have increased her differential preference between the two men as time elapsed; she would not have obliterated the distinctions between them.

Which process predominates—reactance or choice certainty? As will be seen in the section on self-imposed threats, the issue can gain in complexity. Reactance theory appears to be more accurate in research similar to the present example, but it is true that choice-certainty theory has gained clear support in paradigms involving exposure to information prior to decisions. Moreover, there are other theories that can be brought to bear on questions relating to self-imposed threats to freedom, most of which are variations of the choice-certainty idea. For the present it will suffice to note that the case of self-imposed threats is a particularly profitable one from the standpoint of pitting reactance processes against the motivation to achieve certainty or confidence. The details of these juxtaposed theoretical ideas are brought out in the self-imposed threat-to-freedom chapter.

AN OUTLINE OF THE THEORY

The more important ingredients of reactance theory came forth in the examples, but for a review and more complete statement, the elements will be reviewed briefly.

Variables Affecting the Degree of Reactance.

Strength of threat. This was explicated in the example of self-imposed threat, and it should be clear by now that more reactance results as the threat to freedom becomes stronger. The limiting case of a threat is an actual elimination of freedom, which has the greatest power to create reactance.

Presence of freedom. Reactance is aroused through interference with behaviors only when such behaviors can be chosen freely. Instances of this principle were shown in the preceding examples of barriers.

Importance of freedom. As stated in the first example, a freedom is important when the behaviors associated with that freedom have unique instrumental value for satisfaction of important needs, and to the degree that those needs are frequent and central for the person. The more important a freedom, the more reactance is created when that freedom is endangered.

Proportion of freedom threatened. When freedom is defined by a discrete number of decision alternatives, as in the second and third examples, it makes sense to talk about the proportion of freedoms threatened. It is possible to imagine two alternative ways to increase the proportion of freedom threatened. One is to increase the absolute number of behaviors jeopardized, holding constant the size of the original array of free behaviors, and the second is to hold constant the number of behaviors threatened while decreasing the original size of the array. The original statement of reactance theory suggests that reactance arousal is a positive function of the proportion of freedom threatened.

Implication for future threat. Reactance in response to a threat to freedom will be greater to the degree that the threat carries implications for future threats.

Effects of Reactance.

Direct reassertion of freedom through behavior. The central focus of reactance theory is on the motivation to directly reinstate the threatened or eliminated free behavior.

Greater liking for threatened behaviors. Attraction to behaviors threatened with elimination is not conceptually different from engaging in them, but attraction is listed separately because it is a common method of ascertaining the presence of reactance, and because it is the only form of reassertion possible when events make performance of the threatened behavior impossible.

Indirect reassertion of freedom. If a given behavioral freedom is eliminated, that freedom may be restored by the performance of a behavior that would ordinarily imply freedom to perform the one eliminated. For example, performance of a behavior that is either more costly, dangerous, or taboo than the one eliminated would imply to the performer and to the observer that the eliminated behavior can be performed, even though it has been eliminated. This manifestation of reactance carries a definite flavor of "over-reaction," for the performance of a behavior more extreme than the one eliminated does not directly re-establish the loss. It serves instead to prove something about the worth or power of the individual.

Aggression. Aggression toward the source of threat to freedom can be one direct effect of reactance. Such aggression can result even though it does not serve restoration of the freedom. In fact, expressing negative feelings toward the source of restriction can undoubtedly forestall future freedom. Aggression as a concomitant of reactance has been explored in just one study, to be examined in Chapter 15.

2
INTRODUCTION TO
SOCIAL INFLUENCE

The next several chapters cover the topic of effects of attempted social influence. The model for these chapters is the first example in Chapter 1, in which the teen-age boy recoiled from an attempt to change his mind. In the example the attempted influence resulted in a boomerang effect (a change away from the position advocated by the censor), an effect found in some of the research to be reported in these chapters. In other research, reactance processes do not lead to such dramatic effects as boomerang change, but instead, to decreased positive influence. No matter whether the effect is decreased positive influence or actual negative influence, the conceptual idea remains the same: Perceived intent to influence creates reactance, a motivational state that pushes the person away from the position represented by the influence agent.

In some of the research reported the effect of reactance is *attitude* change, while in other research *behavior* change is measured. The distinction between these two effects is not of great theoretical significance, but it is noted because the reader may be interested in focusing on one of the two types of measures. In terms of the examples of Chapter 1, attitude change was exemplified by the censorship case, while behavior change would have been demonstrated if the person who was not allowed to hear the speech had proceeded to expose himself to the censored position.

INTENT TO INFLUENCE AS A SOURCE
OF THREAT TO FREEDOM

Numerous theoretical statements have dealt with pressure to change. Back (1951), Festinger (1950, 1954), French and Raven (1959), Lewin (1947) and numerous others have dealt with the idea of pressure to change, although their emphasis typically has been on positive social influence (i.e., compliance with influence attempts) whereas reactance emphasizes only negative social influences. Throughout this chapter "negative social influence" will designate the phenomenon of a person tending to change in the direction opposite from an influence agent's desires. Festinger (1954) has been explicit on the variable of intent. He discusses factors that lead to uniformity of opinion within groups and delves into such processes as attempts by the group to coerce a deviate to alter his opinions and behaviors to conform to the group. Clearly he assumes that intent to influence on the part of group members can have the end result of bringing individual members into line.

It might be interesting to delve into the question of why a verbal, non-physical influence attempt can bring pressure to change upon individuals. Surely the relationship between an influence attempt and subsequent felt pressure toward change is not something the person is born with. Undoubtedly this is a question to be answered in developmental principles, and we will not undertake it presently. For now, it is sufficient to establish that intent to influence does make people feel pressure to change behaviors, opinions, and abilities under some circumstances, and this point seems well documented both in theory and in research.

Assuming that intended social influence can create pressures toward change, what are the implications for reactance processes? If a person is about to reach for a piece of pie and a second person blurts "Don't take that one," pressure will be created in the direction of rejecting that piece of pie. As experienced by the person choosing, these pressures are felt as urges to avoid the pie, and the pressures are attributable to the source of influence. The stronger the pressure toward change, the greater is the threat to freedom to take any other course of action. Furthermore, the degree of reactance set up by this sensed pressure will be determined by the status of the theoretically-relevant variables spelled out in Chapter 1. For example, if the person feels entirely free and his freedom is important, the negative social influence is likely to be especially strong. In short, when the preconditions for reactance are met, pressure toward change is likely to result in change in the opposite direction.

Social influence can also have a net positive effect that runs counter to reactance processes. In fact, this assumption pervades social psychological theorizing. In cases of boomerang change or resistance to change there will always be forces operating toward positive change (compliance). There have to be such forces in order to arouse reactance. But when freedom is maximized or when the importance of freedom is high, a reactance effect rather than positive influence is likely to be manifested. In other words, to separate reactance effects from positive social influence, variables that are reactance-related will be extremely instrumental, as will be seen in the research.

THEORETICAL VARIABLES: AN OUTLINE
OF THE CHAPTERS TO FOLLOW

At least five of the variables postulated by Brehm have proven to be significant mediators of the relationship between pressure to change and subsequent reactance. Reactance and subsequent negative influence can be exaggerated in intensity, or minimized to zero, depending on the level at which the important mediating variables are operating. There will be considerable discussion of each of these variables, together with relevant research. The purpose of the following chapters is to allow a separate treatment of each of the variables. In the order in which they will be discussed, the variables are the following: strength of threat (Chapter 3), freedom (Chapter 4), importance of freedom (Chapter 5), proportion of freedom threatened (Chapter 6), and implication for future threat (Chapter 7). Chapters 8 and 9 will raise some special issues. Before proceeding with these separate treatments of the theoretical variables there will be a brief discussion of alternative explanations of negative social influence. These explanations, together with reactance theory, can then be evaluated in light of the evidence.

OTHER THEORIES: THE NEGATIVE INFLUENCE AGENT

Cognitive Balance

With the exception of reactance theory almost all of the formulations dealing with resistance to change depend upon the communicator's objectionable qualities. The communicator must be seen as dissimilar, hostile, obnoxious, or more generally as someone with whom the subject would prefer not to associate. A principle that consistently surfaces in these several formulations is a simple notion of cognitive balance, as propounded by Abelson and Rosenberg (1958), Heider (1958), Newcomb (1953), and Osgood and Tannenbaum (1955). If the target of an influence attempt finds himself dissimilar to the source, he will dissociate himself from that source. If the dissociation is accomplished with respect to the issue of the communication, resistance to change and/or negative influence is the result. The following formulations are variations on this cognitive-balance theme: Some focus more on similarity, some on hostility, and some on the source's objectionable qualities.

Miscasting

Cooper and Jones (1969) have proposed an idea that assumes ingratiation tactics (cf. Jones, 1964). When someone desires to win another's approval the approval-seeker will attempt to present himself as associated with the right people. More specifically, if the person finds he has been "miscast," which is to say that he has been associated with an objectionable person, he will proceed to differentiate himself from that person on whatever dimensions are salient to the target of ingratiation. Thus the central idea is consistent with the cognitive-balance notion, but it qualifies the balance idea by the stipulation that a desire to gain approval will motivate the person to dissociate himself from a negatively-valued other. This variation on balance theory will not be discussed further, for it applies in only a limited way to the research. This is because it depends on the subject's desire to win approval from another.

Cognitive Dissonance

Berscheid (1966) reports an experiment consistent with her argument that dissonance is aroused if a person finds that his opinion is similar to that of a second person but that the values relevant to the opinion are not shared. In her experiment subjects were given background information about the relationship between their own values and those of an ostensible subject. The subject was told that the other's values were similar (or dissimilar) to his own on a given topic. After similarity–dissimilarity of values had been manipulated, subjects received a short communication from the other subject (a confederate), which amounted to a statement that a specific position should be held. The position the confederate indicated was always similar to the one the subject had indicated on a premeasure of attitude. Consistent with the idea, there was a shift of opinion away from the position expressed by the dissimilar confederate.

We note a striking similarity to the notion of miscasting, but without the qualification of ingratiation. Berscheid's theoretical notion is a statement of cognitive balance, although she has used the word "dissonance," which carries an important additional overtone. In order to employ dissonance theory unambiguously and in the spirit of the original conception (Brehm & Cohen, 1962; Festinger 1957) it is necessary to know which of the dissonant clusters of cognitions is least resistant to change. That cluster is the one that will show movement. Unfortunately, in Berscheid's experiment and certainly in most of the experimental literature on negative social influence, there is no easy way to assess which of the several possible dissonant elements would be least resistant. Because of this problem Berscheid's use of dissonance theory will not be carried into the following chapters.

Social Equity

Abelson and Miller (1967) have proposed that social equity can sometimes account for the boomerang effect. If a social interaction leads to the statement of an attitude by one person, while a second individual insults or otherwise mistreats the first person in some manner related to the attitude, inequity is established. The person who issues the attitudinal statement simply acts as an honest member of the immediate group, disclosing himself in certain areas. The other person creates inequity by not responding in kind. Instead, he belittle or insults. Abelson and Miller propose that equity can be re-established if the person who is offended adopts a more extreme position. By so doing he returns the insult.

This paradigm assumes that the person creating inequity is simultaneously attempting to change the other person's opinion; thus there is some relation to reactance theory in that the apparent intention to influence is necessary. But other than that, the conception borders on a statement of "provocation-aggression" and does not apply directly to all persuasive situations typically studied.

SUMMARY

There are at least two points of contrast between reactance theory and many of the alternative formulations. First, reactance theory does not require that the source of intent to influence is ill-motivated, reprehensible, hostile, or dissimilar. Of course, it is possible that many of the methods used to create reactance would create a communicator who came across as obnoxious or devious, and this will become an issue shortly. Second, reactance focuses on intent to influence as a central variable, but with the exception of Abelson and Miller none of the other formulations require the presence of an intent to persuade. Typically the balance principle demands only that the subject perceive the other's position, and the balance effects operate from that point.

The discussion of these theoretical approaches is not meant to imply that each of them has broad applicability to the following chapters. For the most part it would take a stretch of the imagination to invoke them, since several of the theories require special assumptions in order to be applied. In particular, the miscasting and cognitive dissonance accounts of negative social influence are difficult to apply directly to paradigms designed around reactance theory, and the major reason for discussing these two frameworks here is to note that under certain conditions they are potentially powerful explanations.

The more general cognitive-balance interpretation (attributable to Heider and others) has a more convincing applicability to some reactance paradigms, as will become evident. For that matter, social equity theory (Abelson and Miller) generally can be invoked in the same places, for the social equity and balance notions are nearly equivalent when applied to negative social influence. Because of this near equivalence, only the balance principle is mentioned from here on.

The following chapters will examine reactance theory, one theoretical variable at a time, with the purpose of showing just how the theory applies to negative social influence. It will be seen that several experiments are crucial in answering theoretically relevant questions—both questions about reactance theory and balance theory. As a side light it might be noted that a fair proportion of the research has direct applicability to social or political questions. Some of the studies in this latter category will be given especially full treatment.

3
STRENGTH OF THREAT TO FREEDOM AND SOCIAL INFLUENCE

Almost any test of reactance theory must manipulate the strength of threat, but the present chapter is unique in that the research discussed here includes no other variables. The paradigm is quite simple. The extent of social influence, or pressure toward change, is varied over two or more levels, then attitude or behavior change is measured.

There is a sense in which this paradigm is too simple. The hypothesis that "increased pressure toward change will result in heightened reactance effects" is probably not testable in and of itself. This is because pressure toward change can have either of two opposing effects as noted in the previous chapter, and unless something definite is known about other variables central to reactance processes, there is no *a priori* way of knowing which of the two effects will result from pressure to change. This is an important point, for a naive reading of reactance theory might conclude that negative social influence should result from any influence attempt, when in fact there is probably just as much theoretical reason to expect positive influence.

Given this ambiguity why would anyone even bother to test reactance theory without also varying some of the mediating variables? The answer is this. If an investigator is looking for negative social influence he will attempt to create conditions conducive to reactance arousal, and thereby have some confidence in his "increased pressure" resulting in negative rather than positive influence. It should not, therefore, be surprising that most of the research included here is supportive of the theory. At the same time it should not be surprising that the unsupportive evidence was gathered by people not interested in finding negative social influence. These latter investigators did not attempt to create the conditions for negative influence, and this is understandable.

The research summarized here has been placed into several empirical categories, simply for the purpose of illustrating the diverse array of social situations leading to threatened freedom. The first of these categories includes theats resulting from explicit statements of intent to influence.

EXPLICIT INTENT TO INFLUENCE

The most straightforward test of reactance theory involves an overt, explicit act of influence. A number of the earlier tests of reactance theory were set up so that a subject had a meaningful choice (or held an attitude of importance), then someone blatantly pushed the subject toward one choice alternative or toward one position on the attitudinal continuum. Several theoretical topics of interest are included under this heading of explicit intent to influence. These will be discussed shortly, following three illustrative experiments.

Weiner (1963) gave gradeschool children a choice among several toys and observed the subject's subsequent ranking of those toys after the subject learned that a peer wanted him to pick a particular toy. The social influence attempt resulted in derogation of the critical toy, consistent with the idea that threat to freedom should motivate the subject to reject the critical toy and become more interested in others.

Brehm and Sensenig (1966) followed a similar format, although the subjects were college students and the choice was between different approaches to an experimental task. For some subjects there was an attempted social influence from a peer, strongly suggesting that the subject should choose a particular approach to the task. Relative to a no-influence control condition, subjects who received this attempted influence tended to reject the recommended task.

An experiment on attitude change by M. L. Brehm reported in Brehm (1966) involved a communication to college students that argued for a stronger program of intercollegiate athletics. Some subjects received the following statement at the end of the persuasive communication: "You, as college students, must inevitably draw the same conclusion." This statement was intended to threaten subjects' freedom to disagree, and consistent with the hypothesis, positive attitude change was less in the presence of this freedom-threatening statement.

These first three experiments are examples of the possible negative effects of social pressure. It should be emphasized that all three studies were designed with the intention of producing reactance, meaning that a clear freedom was built into the situations. In the first two experiments this freedom was defined in terms of a choice, and in the third it was assumed that subjects felt free to come to their own conclusions on the issue of intercollegiate athletics. Nonetheless, there was no completely firm basis in any of those experiments for expecting reactance forces to outweigh compliance forces. Had the freedoms not been sufficiently important, or had other reactance-producing elements been insufficient, the pressure may easily have created a compliance effect. To illustrate the possibility of this compliance effect, two experiments will be mentioned.

In the first experiment (Mills & Aronson, 1965) the communicator was either ugly or beautiful, and she either announced her explicit desire to persuade the audience prior to communicating to them, or she did not. The intent-to-persuade manipulation made a difference only when the communicator was physically attractive, and the difference was such that persuasion increased under high intent to persuade. The second experiment (Mills, 1966) was similar, although the communicator's likableness was varied rather than physical attractiveness. Again, given a likable communicator, intent to persuade heightened persuasion.

The results are at face value contrary to reactance theory and underscore a point registered earlier. Any test of the hypothesis that social pressure will have negative, rather than positive, influence is inherently ambiguous because the factors necessary for reactance arousal must be at a sufficiently high level before such pressure will have negative effects. The difficulty, of course, is that "sufficiently high" is inherently ambiguous. Without an adequate pretesting of an experimental design it is difficult to know whether or not the vital factors (e.g., freedom and importance of that freedom) are present in adequate degree. Possibly the attitude in these last two experiments, the issue of general vs. specialized education, was not of much importance to subjects, but this is mere speculation. As will be seen in subsequent chapters, this ambiguity is minimized or eliminated when other theoretical variables are used.

Disregarding the reactance question temporarily, there is some good evidence for the cognitive-balance interpretation in Mills' experiment. Not only did the likable communicator gain increased positive influence by stating her explicit intent to influence, but interestingly, the *un*likable communicator's statement of intent to influence had exactly the opposite effect. Among subjects confronted with an unlikable communicator there was more agreement with her when she *did not* state her intention to influence than when she did. Subjects appear to follow the wishes of someone with whom they would like to be associated, but they act in a contrary manner toward someone who does not win their favor.

The first three experiments discussed might also be amenable to a cognitive-balance interpretation, assuming that the influence agent's high-pressure influence attempt rendered him unlikable or distasteful. This cognitive-balance interpretation is addressed directly in the Worchel and Arnold (1973) experiment discussed later in this chapter and in the Sensenig and Brehm (1968) experiment discussed in Chapter 7. Both of those studies make the point that reactance can lead to its predicted effects without the mediation of cognitive-balance processes, although to invoke those findings in the present context may be presumptuous. For the present it should be noted only that a demand can have reactance-like effects, but that those effects are potentially amenable to a Heiderian interpretation.

Simultaneous Threats to Freedom

The original theory says nothing in particular about dual, simultaneous, or repeated threats. At face value there is no reason to think that two independent threats would have effects qualitatively different from a strengthened single threat. The general notion that reactance is a monotonic function of strength of threat can, in theory, be applied to the effect of multiple threats.

At least two distinct outcomes of simultaneous threats are conceivable. The first possibility, in line with a straightforward reading of the theory, is that the effects would simply be additive. Translating this literally, if Threat A by itself produced a negative social influence effect of −3, and Threat B by itself did the same, their combination should result in a change of −6. The second possibility assumes that two simultaneous threats have a multiplicative effect, such that the effect of combining Threats A and B would be a net change somewhat greater than −6. This might happen if a person is sensitized to infringements on his freedom once he is confronted by an initial threat. In this sensitized state he would be especially likely to react strongly to subsequent threats. With this background two relevant studies will be described.

Heller, Pallak, and Picek (1973) report an experiment that uses elements from the Brehm and Sensenig experiment. Subjects expected to write an essay on a controversial topic, and they expected some freedom of choice about which position to take in the essay. Two independent manipulations of threat to freedom were brought into play by a confederate. The first of these consisted of a manipulation of the confederate's general desire to influence people on the topic in question. In the "low threat" condition he indicated no particular desire to influence, but in the "high threat" condition he told the subject, "I decided that I should persuade as many people as I can. . ." The second threat manipulation was focused directly on the subject's freedom to choose. In the "high threat" condition the confederate said, "I've decided that you must write your essay against the establishment of. . ." The confederate was much less demanding in the "low threat" condition.

The Heller et al. dependent measure is instructive regarding the relationship between threat to freedom of choice and manifestations of the motivation to regain the freedom. The measure was the subject's attitude toward the issue on which he was to write. Clearly the most direct manifestation of the threatened freedom in this case would have been an overt attempt to write an essay opposed to that suggested by the confederate, but it is important to note that one manifestation of that motivation is the subject's subsequent attitude on the issue. If reactance creates a motivation to regain the freedom to choose Side A of the issue, the subject's attitude should shift toward Side A. This is precisely what happened, as evidenced in Table 1. A positive mean indicates attitude change toward the recommended position, and a negative mean represents a boomerang (reactance) effect. The interaction between the two types of threats was significant. These effects are due largely to the substantial negative change (–9.00) in the high-high condition. Evidently the two threats combined in multiplicative fashion.

In summary, the Heller et al. experiment shows that two simultaneous threats seem to have a multiplicative effect. Second, the experiment spells out the important theoretical connection between threat to freedom of choice and subsequent attitude toward the events entailed in that choice.

The other recent experiment was performed by Doob and Zabrack (1971), a field study of reactance processes. It contains two independent threats just as in the previous experiment. Doob and Zabrack mailed 200 people questionnaires to fill out and return, varying the instructions sent along with the questionnaires. The idea behind the experiment was to arouse reactance in two different ways: first, by using forceful language in the instructions, and second, by including in the request a small amount of money as additional pressure to comply with the instructions.

Subjects received in the mail a 15-item questionnaire to be completed and returned. In the No Reactance condition the accompanying instructions were

TABLE 1

ATTITUDE CHANGE

Second threat variable	First threat variable	
	High	Low
High	-9.00^{a}	1.00
Low	.25	1.25

[a]Negative change represents attitude change away from the position advocated by the confederate.

polite and requested that the form be returned within three days. For half of the No Reactance subjects 20¢ was included, "as a small token of our appreciation."

The enclosed directions in the Reactance condition were somewhat more forceful:

> This is part of a mail survey which we have been conducting in various areas of the country on a variety of topics. You must fill out this questionnaire and return it immediately in the stamped addressed envelope.

For half of the Reactance subjects 20¢ was enclosed and the following comment was added to the previous quote: "To ensure prompt return we have enclosed twenty cents."

A direct method of reasserting one's behavioral freedom in response to a survey request is to return the blank questionnaire to the sender with the money, if it had been included. As might be expected, most of the reactance resulted in the Reactance–20¢ condition, in which 11% of the subjects returned the blank questionnaire plus money. This 11% was significantly greater than the percentage of blank returns in any other condition ($p < .05$), supporting a clear derivation from the theory.

Conceptually, this experiment is identical to the study just discussed. The effect here was produced by the combination of two independent sources of pressure—strong language and monetary push. There is some evidence here for a multiplicative effect when two threats are combined, although the statistical evidence is strongest in the Heller et al. experiment. The two experiments together indicate that threats may well combine nonadditively, and as far as theoretical explanations are concerned, the sensitivity notion set forth above may offer an adequate account. In the context of the Heller et al. procedure it is quite easy to imagine the sensitivity processes operating. Some of the subjects were first confronted with a confederate who indicated that "I should persuade as many people as I can," and certainly from that point on they should have been especially sensitive to any further freedom-threatening gestures and remarks.[1]

What Makes for a High-Pressure Communicator?

The next experiment, by Brehm and Brehm (reported in Brehm, 1966), is especially instructive concerning a primary theoretical point. Earlier it was noted that negative social influence via reactance arousal can result only to the degree that the subject feels a definite pressure to comply. Ironically, negative change should result from strong felt pressure toward positive change.

---

[1]It is worth mentioning that a multiplicative effect of two threats is also demonstrated in studies by Schwartz (at the end of this chapter) and by Liberman and Wicklund (Chapter 9).

The procedure differed in one major respect from the previous experiment by M. L. Brehm. A communicator-power variable was introduced by describing the communicator either as a prominent educator or as a high-school student who had won an award for his essay on teaching machines. The high-school student was said to have won an award because it was desirable for the expertise of the two communicators to be approximately equivalent while their power varied. The communication was reasonable, contained various facts, and was unemotional. It ended with a statement strongly advocating teaching machines, and in the High Threat condition the following comment was added: "Students at the University of Washington must by all means agree."

The results are tabulated in Table 2 in terms of frequencies of subjects who showed no change, moved toward, or moved away from the communicator. From inspection of the frequencies it is apparent that the two types of communicators brought about markedly different effects. When the message came from a professor the High Threat condition produced slightly more negative than positive change, while there was predominantly positive change in the Low Threat condition. This High-Low Threat difference within the "professor" condition was statistically significant. By way of contrast, the threat variable made very little difference when the source was a high-school student. The High-Low Threat differences are not significantly different between the "professor" and "high-school student" conditions, but the trend toward a differential pattern is worth some discussion.

TABLE 2
OPINION CHANGE AS A FUNCTION OF COMMUNICATOR AND THREAT

Communicator	Opinion response		
	Toward	No change	Away
Professor			
Low Threat	13	3	5
High Threat	6	1	8
High-school student			
Low Threat	15	0	6
High Threat	12	0	2

Brehm (1966) indicates that this pattern is inconsistent with an original expectation that a threat from an inappropriate source (the student) would create more reactance than a threat from a supposed legitimate, high-prestige source. Obviously this did not occur. Brehm entertains the possibility that the threat statement from the high-school student carried no impact. Subjects indicated that the communicator's recommendations were inappropriate only in the case of the student issuing the strong threat, and this rating of inappropriateness may have reflected the subject's failure to take the high-school student's threat seriously. Perhaps a younger person who demands compliance may appear silly and ineffectual, which is to say that his threat is vacuous, will be viewed as out of place, and can be disregarded easily.

Conceptually, just what was manipulated? The variable could be labeled "prestige," "age," "authority," or numerous other factors, but there is a more theoretical way to look at the variable. If the high-school student's threat was hollow, this probably means that his demand created few, if any, pressures to comply, and if we consider the life histories of the subjects this begins to make sense. In any person's history it is the authority, the prestige figure, and the older person who has the power to back up threats. By generalizing from numerous earlier instances of communications from authorities the subject should have experienced a stronger pressure to change when the professor addressed them, even though there was no physical threat in the situation. In summary, the person who characterizes authority, in the sense of ability to follow up a threat, will create the most reactance.

FOCUSING ATTENTION ON PERSUASIVE FEATURES OF THE COMMUNICATION

In several experiments to be described without great detail the experimental manipulation gave subjects different orientations toward speeches. The attention of some subjects was directed toward the speech so that they should have perceived more intent to influence. This manipulation is directly analogous to a variation in explicit intent to influence, because the differential focusing causes subjects to be differentially cognizant of the intent to persuade. It should be noted that the focusing-of-attention variable is not a theoretical variable of reactance theory. Focused attention toward persuasive intent is simply one of several interesting ways to bring a person to perceive a threat to his freedom.

In an experiment by Allyn and Festinger (1961) subjects encountered a persuasive communication that ran contrary to their own attitudes, but before exposure they were given a differential orientation. Some subjects were told to attend to the speaker's personality, while others were warned that the speaker would take a definite stand on the issue that was in disagreement with their own. It seems rather likely that subjects in the latter condition strongly suspected an intent to influence, while in the other condition any suspicion of intent to persuade would have been gathered through actual exposure and certainly should not have been as great. Consistent with the above reasoning, the persuasive attempt was less successful when subjects' attention was trained on the issue.

Festinger and Maccoby (1964) conducted three experiments conceptually similar to the Allyn and Festinger experiment. In one condition subjects viewed a movie in which the sound track and picture were well-coordinated. The talk was about fraternities, and the speaker was pictured throughout in an appropriate setting. In the "distraction" version of the film the talk was accompanied on the screen by an entertaining comedy dealing with a painter. Consistent with the Allyn and Festinger study, more attitude change resulted when subjects were distracted. This is consistent with the reactance interpretation in that the perceived intent to influence should be a direct function of the subject's attention to the communication. If he doesn't attend to it, he can hardly feel the pressure to change emanating from it.

Walster and Festinger (1962) conducted two experiments that manipulated the focus of attention in a slightly different way from that of the previous studies. A situation was constructed so that some subjects would not necessarily think the communicators were aware of their presence, while other subjects knew that the communicators were aware of the audience of subjects. This seems to be an especially good manipulation of the subject's attention toward persuasive intent. If the communicator doesn't appear to be cognizant of his audience, the audience cannot very well assume that he intends to persuade. The results are again consistent with the prediction, especially for subjects highly involved in the issue used in the persuasion. When the communicators were depicted as aware of the presence of an audience there was less persuasion than when they were ostensibly unaware.

Finally, there is a short line of research on the effects of forewarning the audience of the persuasive nature of the communication. In experiments by Kiesler and Kiesler (1964) and Dean, Austin, and Watts (1971), subjects were warned at the outset of the communication that it was a persuasive attempt. As would be expected, the persuasive impact was diminished by such a forewarning. Among the various possible effects a forewarning might have, it does seem clear that forewarned subjects' attention should have been called to the persuasive content of the speech.

Summary

Whether the subject's attention was drawn toward the persuasive intent (Allyn and Festinger, Dean et al., Kiesler and Kiesler) or away from the persuasive intent (Festinger and Maccoby, Walster and Festinger), the conceptual point is the same: Persuasive appeals lose power to the degree that the person's attention is focused toward aspects of the communication designed to manipulate him. This research is especially interesting from the standpoint of reactance theory, because it suggests that with a communication held constant and communicator's characteristics not varied, reactance is a direct function of the amount of time a subject spends in dwelling on the intent to persuade him. If he can be kept from thinking about the intent to persuade, reactance forces become insignificant.

Reactance theory aside, it is only fair to note that there is another perfectly good explanation for these forewarning effects. There is the notion that counterarguing is inhibited by taking the subject's attention away from persuasive elements. This idea applies comfortably to the body of this research, and to make a strong case for reactance processes it would be necessary to take either of two tacks: (*a*) The processes supposed to mediate counterarguing could be shown not to take place differentially between conditions. For example, if it were possible to tap into the amount of counterarguing going on in the Festinger and Maccoby experiments, and if the conditions did not differ in quantity of counterarguing, there would be good justification for giving precedence to reactance processes. (*b*) The ideal experiment in the focusing-of-attention area would entail a prior manipulation of whether or not subjects felt free to reject the viewpoint of the communication. Conditions would be arranged so that half the subjects felt such freedom and half did not. Then these two conditions would be subdivided along the lines of one of the manipulations used in the focusing-of-attention research. The communication would draw a particular conclusion, and agreement with the communication would be measured. If reactance were responsible for the effect, subjects should resist influence to the extent that their attention is turned toward intent (i.e., if they are forewarned), but this effect should operate only among subjects who have prior freedom to reject the position advocated. Within the hypothetical no-freedom condition, the focusing-of-attention (forewarning) variable should make no difference. As it turns out, such an experiment has been performed by Jones and Brehm and is reported in Chapter 4.

COMMUNICATOR'S INVESTMENT IN ISSUE

If someone appears completely ego-involved in an issue, or behavior, others are often wary of his comments about that issue. The ego-involved individual is often defensive and goes to great lengths not only to defend his position but also to convince others of the correctness of his behavior. Such ego-involvement, or personal interest on the part of a communicator, should exaggerate reactance processes. Not only does an ego-involved communicator appear eager to persuade, but he can often be depended upon to engage in repeated influence attempts. There are numerous ways in which a person can become ego-involved, and Brock (1965) has examined one of these in an ingenious field experiment.

The experiment took place in a paint store, where the usual customers unknowingly served as subjects. Once the customer had indicated that he desired to buy such-and-such gallons of paint, the salesman (who doubled as an experimenter) went with him to the cash register, and then the manipulation began. Keeping in mind the quantity desired by the customer, the salesman said that recently he had occasion to purchase ____ gallons of a *different type* of paint, and that it had worked "beautifully." This was the essence of the persuasive appeal. Inserted in the blank above should be the number of gallons indicated by the salesman, which was either identical to the number the customer wanted or else 20 times that quantity. At this point we should reconsider the procedure, which appears to contain a variation in perceived intent to influence via the communicator's ego-involvement.

The customer confronted with a salesman who has bought only a gallon or two of the recommended paint might assume that the salesman has no great investment in the product. It is as though the salesman has simply been experimenting, trying a gallon or two at a time, and never really committing himself firmly. But a salesman claiming to have purchased 20 gallons is on the spot. He is apparently committed to the type of paint, and the customer would perceive him as someone with a strong personal investment. What does all of this have to do with intent to influence and pressure to change?

First, the customer will suppose that he stands a chance of insulting the committed salesman by not purchasing the recommended type of paint. This supposition would be a source of pressure to change and a source of reactance. Second, the customer is likely to think that the persuasion attempt will be longer and more relentless from the committed salesman—again leading to more reactance. Finally, the fact that the salesman said he purchased a greater quantity directly implies to the customer that he could benefit from purchasing a similar quantity, and again, pressure to change is increased. From any of these alternative reasonings, or from their combination, the manipulation makes perfectly good sense seen from the perspective of reactance theory. In fact, the actual results also make sense from this perspective. Customers were more likely to switch to the recommended type of paint when the salesman's ego-involvement was low.

In summary, the influence agent's ego-involvement or personal investment in the issue can be a prime source of perceived intent to influence. It is likely that this variety of reactance manipulation is quite common in everyday occurrences of reactance arousal.

CENSORSHIP

Among the most blatant attempts to coerce people into designated attitudinal positions are efforts to censor communications, whether through the newspapers, television, or public speeches. Censorship inevitably allows the potential audience to infer both the censor's feelings about the matter involved and his desire to influence. Undoubtedly reactance could be created by a person's mere knowledge that someone intends to influence him, but when the intent to influence is accompanied by deceit, manipulation, and overt attempts to convey one side of the issue, the felt pressure to change will be greatly magnified.

Several forms of censorship can be ordered according to their effectiveness in creating reactance.

(*1*) The first of these is a limiting minimal case of censorship and entails the mere deletion or threat of deletion of a message, where the deletion is not accompanied by a perceived intent to influence. An obvious example is interference with a televised political speech due to difficulties in transmission. Unless the viewer thinks that someone intentionally tampered with the system of transmission, he will feel no strong pressure to change his feelings about the issue one way or another.

(*2*) If a communication is censored because of one element, such as obscenity, there is little reason to expect the listener to feel his freedom threatened with respect to a second element, given that the second element is an attitudinal issue. An audience expects to view a pro-war movie, but before the showing it is cancelled because of various profanities scattered throughout. In this case the possibility of hearing profanity may become more attractive. However, the pro- vs. anti-war issue should remain unaffected by the censorship, unless the audience happens to conclude that censorship for the sake of profanity was simply a sham for keeping them from exposure to pro-war sentiments. Undoubtedly this latter alternative is frequently observed, for once a censor acts on a communication with the intent of keeping it from the audience, they can easily attribute his behavior to any specific aspect of the censored material.

(*3*) Reactance will be most strongly aroused when the censor explicitly prohibits exposure because of a particular issue. Given that a certain viewpoint is intentionally kept from them, the audience members should experience reactance and show a subsequent shift of attitude in the direction of the position that was to be defended or advocated in the presentation. In the experiments to be reviewed, reactance effects are found primarily in conditions of this nature.

Obviously reactance cannot claim to be the sole explanation of boomerang attitude-change effects resulting from censorship. The following is one of the more obvious general accounts of such effects. If a communication is suddenly removed from public exposure, the person who expected to see or hear it is very likely to infer that there was something especially unique, exotic, or persuasive about it. Suppose a college student builds up the expectation that he can hear a speech favoring Black separatism, to be given by a notorious radical. Shortly before the speaker's scheduled appearance the university unexpectedly bans the talk on the grounds that the viewpoint taken is "uncivilized." The student may conclude from this that the speaker would have been especially persuasive. Otherwise, why would the censor deal with him as though his thoughts were dangerous? Once persuasiveness is imputed to the censored speech it is a short leap to argue that the student will alter his opinion in the direction of the anticipated position, simply because the act of censorship has rendered that a powerful position. This process would seem especially likely if the audience knew that the censor had something to lose by the persuasive presentation of views contrary to his own.

A related reason for a boomerang effect focuses on the censor's own position rather than on the one to be represented in the communication. If someone finds it necessary to go to such devious means as censorship of a disagreeable position, the audience might well conclude that the censor's position is weak and indefensible, with resulting attitude change away from the censor's position. Again the explanation assumes an inference process based on the censor's behavior, whereas reactance theory focuses on the threat to freedom produced by the censor's manipulative behavior.

The first experimental study of censorship was conducted by Wicklund and Brehm (1967). Two weeks before the experimental sessions, junior high-school students of both sexes were given a premeasure on the issue of whether or not the voting age should be lowered from 21 to 18. Four days before the experimental manipulations the students were led to expect they would hear a speaker support the position that was popular with them. Their teachers told them there was to be an assembly at which a Mr. Feiffer from the State Board of Elections would deliver a school-assembly talk advocating a lowered voting age.

The manipulations were carried out on the morning of the scheduled assembly and took the form of an announcement read to the students. This announcement took either of two forms:

(Censorship condition) The assembly originally scheduled for today has been cancelled permanently. Mr. Hopkins from the County School Board has cancelled the assembly because the speaker, Mr. Feiffer, was to have spoken in favor of lowering the voting age to 18. Mr. Hopkins does not feel that junior high-school students should hear a talk that is in favor of lowering the voting age.

TABLE 3

PERCENTAGES OF SUBJECTS WHO CHANGED TOWARD
THE SPEAKER'S POSITION[a]

Condition	School 1	School 2
Censorship	79.5 (N = 39)	50.0 (N = 16)
No censorship	56.8 (N = 37)	38.1 (N = 21)

[a] Same as away from the censor's position.

(No Censorship condition) Mr. Feiffer, who was to speak today on why
the voting age should be lowered to 18, has suddenly become ill.
Therefore, the assembly which was originally scheduled for today has
been cancelled permanently.

Immediately after the announcement an attitude postmeasure was given. In
Table 3 the attitude-change data are presented in terms of percentages of
subjects who changed toward the speaker's position. An inspection of the
table reveals that there was more change toward the speaker in the Censorship condition than in the No Censorship condition, and further, the difference was similar for the two schools used in the research. Combining the
data from the two schools by a method reported in Maxwell (1961, p. 77),
there is a reliable difference between conditions (C.R. $= 2.14, p = .03$).

Ashmore, Ramchandra, and Jones (1971) carried out an experiment
similar to the above. All subjects expected to hear a speech, although for
some subjects the speech upheld their own opinions and for other subjects
the speech supported an opposing opinion. Relative to a No Censor control,

TABLE 4

MEAN ATTITUDE CHANGE[a]

Censor other position	No censor	Censor own position
−2.00	−0.17	1.75

[a] A positive score indicates movement toward the end of the scale initially endorsed by the
subject.

opinions shifted in the direction of the anticipated speech when it was announced that the dean of the college would not allow the taped speech to be played. These results are summarized in Table 4.

Summary of Wicklund-Brehm and Ashmore et al.

The two experiments support the theoretical ideas taken from reactance theory, although certain qualifications should be noted. First, subjects may have imputed persuasiveness to the communication as a result of the act of censorship, as discussed above. Second, subjects may have concluded from the censorship that the censor's position was indefensible, and that he found it necessary to resort to questionable tactics in order to prevent students from disagreeing with him. This being the case, they would have shifted away from his indefensible and tenuous position.

There is one more alternative explanation that focuses on perceived characteristics of the censor. Assuming the general operation of the balance principle, subjects in both experiments could have reacted to a disliked censor by dissociating themselves from his position, which is the same as moving in the direction of the censored speaker. This balance interpretation remains somewhat tenable in light of the censorship research discussed thus far, for there are no data on liking for the censor.

In summary, the two experiments taken together indicate that censorship of a potentially persuasive communication can have a boomerang effect, defined as the potential audience members shifting their views toward the position represented by the censored material.

Reactance Theory vs. Balance Theory: Interpreting Effects of Censorship

Worchel and Arnold (1973) set out to separate reactance processes from cognitive-balance processes within a censorship paradigm. Since their procedure was quite elaborate, just the crucial aspects of it will be covered here. The idea was to vary the characteristics of the censor between positive and negative, allowing a direct test of the balance interpretation. If cognitive balance is the basis of the censorship effect, the negative censor should be more effective.

College students were told by an experimenter that she had intended to play them a tape-recorded talk advocating the exclusion of police from college campuses. The subjects found, however, that they would not hear the talk, for one of three reasons. In the Positive Censor condition the experimenter said that the campus YM-YWCA group had prevented the playing of the talk, in the Negative Censor condition the censoring group was the John Birch Society, and in the Neutral Censor condition a broken tape recorder was held responsible. (It should be noted that the censorship in the

TABLE 5

MEAN ATTITUDES ON THE POLICE-ON-CAMPUS ISSUE

	Positive censor	Negative censor	Neutral censor	No censor
Amount of agreement with censor's position	6.88[a]	5.53	7.39	9.38

[a] A low number represents agreement with the viewpoint of the speech; a high number represents agreement with the apparent position of the censor.

latter condition has no possible basis in a censor's intent to influence.) Finally, there was a No Censor condition in which there was never any mention of a tape-recorded speech nor of a censor. Subjects in all conditions were given the relevant attitude measure following the manipulation.

Table 5 shows the attitude results, in which the three combined censorship conditions are significantly different from the No Censor group. No significant differences appeared among the censor conditions, which suggests that cognitive balance is a somewhat implausible explanation of these results. There is just one difficulty in the data, and that is in regard to the Neutral Censor condition. The Wicklund and Brehm No Censorship condition was quite similar to Worchel and Arnold's Neutral Censor condition, in that the speech was eliminated for accidental reasons, and not due to intended influence. This being the case it is surprising that Worchel and Arnold's Neutral Censor condition produced so much agreement with the censored position. Perhaps one reason for this is that the accidental elimination acts as a barrier, producing an increased desire to hear the communication and consequent attitude change. If this is true, the same may have occurred in the Wicklund and Brehm experiment, and such a process would have weakened the differential effect in that study. In short, the control condition in the Wicklund and Brehm experiment was probably a highly conservative one, because accidental elimination also appears to create somewhat of a "censorship" effect.

Adding all three studies together the evidence for a reactance-theory interpretation of censorship becomes stronger. Any interpretations based on the censor's characteristics seem to be ruled out, although discussion of censorship should be left with one reservation. It is still possible that the results of these studies were due to the imputed persuasiveness of unheard communications, and reactance theory should not be viewed as the exclusive interpretation as long as this alternative remains viable.

Summary

It has been shown that censorship provides a viable and rather strong source of threat to freedom. Explicit intent to influence, focused attention on persuasive content, communicator's investment or ego-involvement, and censorship all appear to constitute sources of reactance arousal in a social setting. At this point a fifth and final variety of social pressure will be examined. This last one assumes that important freedoms can be threatened when someone asks for help.

HELPING BEHAVIOR: THE REACTANCE-AROUSING EFFECTS OF DEPENDENCE

Individual acts of helping are subject to the forces of reactance just as the free-choice behaviors dealt with in the research reported previously. If a potential donor or philanthropist is confronted with a decision of whether or not to give, his choice can be altered by threatening his freedom appropriately. If there are pressures toward benevolence, reactance will lead him to refuse favors, and if there are pressures away from giving, reactance will tend to turn him into a giver. Such effects operate in contrast to a "social responsibility norm" (Berkowitz & Daniels, 1963, 1964; Goranson & Berkowitz, 1966), which indicates that a person will benefit others when duty calls.

It is commonly assumed that the needy are also the helped. The sight of someone suffering is thought to set off acts of charity and benevolence, and it is a corollary of this common assumption that the amount of help given will be positively related to the amount of help required. Examples of this corollary are abundant enough. Out of the thousands of afflictions people encounter each year, just a few of the relatively incapacitating ones are given prominence in terms of campaigns for voluntary donations. Apparently it is assumed that a request to help a heart attack victim will be more successful than a request to help someone with a mild case of pneumonia, but reactance theory implies that the pneumonia case or even milder afflictions will sometimes benefit more from requests.

The reactance analysis of helping behavior is no different from its consideration of other types of social influence. The act of attempted social influence will normally have two opposing effects: one operating toward compliance, the other away from compliance. The strength of the resistance forces is determined by the variables that lead to reactance, and in the following study by Schwartz (1970) the preconditions for reactance arousal seem to have been satisfied. Subjects should have felt a good deal of prior freedom regarding the behavior in question, and given the context this freedom was highly important.

Subjects were asked to join a pool of possible bone-marrow donors who supposedly were waiting to aid a young woman. Pressure to join the pool was manipulated in two independent ways: (a) The purported need of the woman was varied over three levels so that subjects either thought she was slightly, moderately, or greatly in need of a bone marrow transplant. (b) The subject was told either that there was 1/1000 of a chance that his marrow would match the woman's or else 1/25 of a chance. In the latter case (1/25) he should have felt more pressure to commit himself to the pool of donors.

Although common sense might dictate a direct relationship between the woman's need and subjects' willingness to donate, such an effect occurred only when there was 1/1000 chance of taking marrow. When the odds were higher (1 chance in 25) the relationship between the woman's need and the willingness to volunteer was curvilinear. Volunteering increased, going from low need to moderate need, but when her need was great (her life depended on it) there was a decline in willingness to join the donor pool.

In short, it appears as though reactance effects occurred only when each of the pressures toward compliance was at a maximum level. This effect is reminiscent of the effect of combined threats noted earlier in the context of an experiment by Heller et al. There appears to be a qualitative leap when two threats are maximal, such that the effect is greater than would be expected from summing the two threats taken individually.

This final variety of social threat to freedom seems particularly striking because of its implications for human nature. Apparently reactance can interfere with benevolence, and ironically, the need to preserve and regain freedom may be greatest under those conditions in which we are called upon to save lives. Theoretically it makes sense, for a request to save someone's life can easily serve as the strongest possible social pressure. But from the standpoint of someone who believes in a benevolent human nature, the resistance exhibited by Schwartz' subjects is probably surprising.

CHAPTER SUMMARY

The primary purpose of this chapter was to illustrate the variety of ways in which intent to influence can be created. The most obvious of these is the first, explicit intent to influence. The existence of several others, some of a noncommon sense nature, contributes to the generality of the theory.

This chapter has been used for two other ends. The first is theoretical, and three issues of some importance were discussed: (a) The consequences of two simultaneous threats to a freedom, (b) the notion that reactance can occur only when there is felt pressure to comply (discussed in the context of the Brehm and Brehm research), and (c) the viability of the cognitive-balance interpretation of negative social influence.

The other end was of an applied nature. This excursion into types of threats has been an opportunity to indicate that the theory has been taken into areas of direct social applicability. Most notable is the censorship and helping research. Other instances of direct application will come up at various points throughout the book.

4
FREEDOM AND SOCIAL INFLUENCE

"Freedom" is the central concept of reactance theory, yet it is the theoretical concept most often misused, owing perhaps to the many uses given the term in everyday parlance. The major kind of misuse of the term can best be illustrated by the following "application" of reactance theory.

It has been said that the oppressed should experience more reactance than anyone. Their freedom is kept at a low ebb by a plethora of discriminatory tactics. They are neither hired nor educated equally, and they are ruled out of most social exchange. Therefore, reactance theory is a good explanation of their protesting and rioting.

There is an important and incorrect assumption running through this and similar examples. The assumption is that reactance will result whenever someone is pushed around, discriminated against, or treated unfairly. Theoretically, this assumption is completely incorrect. The person who has been ordered, castigated, and dominated his entire life probably never came to expect many freedoms in the first place. If he ever did develop the expectation of freedom, his repeated subjugation should have quickly eliminated that expectation. The main point is this: The theory in no way assumes that everyone is born with an expectation of being free in every possible domain. Rather, freedoms in particular areas develop through the experience of being able to act freely, or possibly through social conventions. A 10-year-old may feel little if any freedom to choose among different types of contraceptives—one reason being that he has never built up an expectation of freedom, and the other reason being that society does not condone this freedom for 10-year-olds.

In talking about freedom within the context of the theory it is helpful to speak in terms of particular sets of options as being free or unfree, rather than using the notion "freedom" more generally. For example, it makes little theoretical sense to speak of a "free person," since everybody is free with respect to certain behavioral options, but not free in other respects. The

39

young man just described probably has freedom to name his own brand of ice cream or to choose his own friends, but he would not have a firm expectation of freedom in areas involving sex, large amounts of money, or other adult functions.

It may also be noted that a freedom once acquired is not necessarily a freedom for evermore. This point can be illustrated by showing what should happen when a freedom is restricted repeatedly. Reactance can be aroused in the young man who has freedom to choose ice cream brands quite easily. Simply force him to eat a given brand. But if this same brand is forced upon him time after time, there will be a point at which he will no longer expect the freedom to choose. In short, he is no longer free, thus not in a position to experience reactance. Reactance theory does not carry specific parameters that would tell us precisely how many consecutive restrictions it takes before the expectation of free choice dwindles, but the central idea is that the freedom will dissipate eventually.

Experimentally, how do we know when a person is free? With almost no exceptions this very simple procedure has been employed: Some subjects are told they are free to choose from an array of alternatives, while other subjects are instructed that they have no freedom of choice with respect to that array. Following this straightforward manipulation of freedom, differential reactance should then be expected when the subject is constrained to take certain of the alternatives. Specifically, the free individual should become motivated from reactance to reject the items he is forced to take, and at the same time he will attempt to regain alternatives that were ruled out. The behavior of the initially unfree person will be markedly different. There should be no systematic motivation to reject or regain any of the alternatives, for those alternatives never were components of a free choice. In short, the initially unfree person will not experience reactance.

The first experiment reported in this chapter, by Jones, illustrates how freedom is manipulated in this way. In his experiment the behavioral options are helping vs. not helping, and some subjects are led to expect a free choice between these alternatives.

The method of creating freedom which was just described works perfectly well for overt, behavioral options, but how should freedom of *attitudes* be dealt with? It is difficult to conceive of a person not feeling free to hold any attitude, for attitudes are a private matter and freedom to select among the different positions on an issue cannot readily be created or "uncreated" by an experimenter or society. Once a person is aware that a position can be taken on some particular dimension of attitude, he almost necessarily feels free to adopt that position. After all, there is nothing to stop him from doing so. But perhaps "once a person is aware that a position can be taken" is the key to freedom of attitudes. It may be that awareness of a possible position is

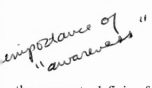

the answer to defining freedom of attitudes. Some elaboration will help on this point.

There are many issues on which we would never imagine holding certain positions. For example, many people have never considered the possibility of holding the opinion that daily tooth-brushing is useless, or that unrestricted homicide is a viable route to population control. Such positions exist logically, but people are effectively unaware of the positions. In essence they have adopted a restricted attitudinal continuum, defined perhaps by "teeth should be brushed four times daily" and "teeth should be brushed once a day." "Toothbrushing is useless" is not included on the attitudinal dimension. Such restricted conceptions of attitudinal dimensions are probably common and would occur whenever practical experience systematically leads us away from thinking about certain logical end points of the continuum.

It should be possible to vary freedom of attitude by locating an issue that is truncated by most people, and then making some people aware of the previously "left out" portion of the continuum. This is what McGuire (1961) has done in his research on cultural truisms. He has found issues that are typically truncated, then he has informed people of the previously "unknown" position. In terms of reactance theory, people who are made aware of the previously left-off portion of the continuum should feel the freedom to hold a position within that recently discovered segment. In contrast, people who remain unaware of that segment should feel no such freedom.

This method of varying freedom has been effected by Jones and Brehm (1970) in the second experiment reported in this chapter. This is one of the few places in the book where this type of freedom manipulation has been employed, and it is important because it is a clear alternative to the more common choice–no-choice variation.

FREEDOM MANIPULATED BY CHOICE–NO-CHOICE INSTRUCTIONS

In this experiment by R. A. Jones (1970) there are three variables. The first two, amount of threat and freedom, have already been explored, but the third deserves some comment. "Implication for further threat" is a variable to be explored in Chapter 7, but its essence can be summarized by noting that reactance will be greater when a threat to freedom has implications for future threats. If two threats are identical but one of them carries an implication for future threats, reactance will thereby be enhanced.

Jones' subjects were confronted with the opportunity to volunteer to help a graduate student with some research, and the measure of compliance was simply the amount of time volunteered by subjects. The three experimental variables were manipulated as follows. (a) One of these was the subject's freedom with respect to helping: Some subjects were led to think they were entitled to refuse to help if they elected to do so, while others were made to feel an obligation to give at least minimal assistance. (*b*) A second variable was the dependence of the person requesting the assistance: The subject was told either that numerous subjects were needed to help, or else that just a few would be needed. The easiest way to conceptualize this second variable is in terms of the strength of threat, in that the subject who understands that numerous subjects will be needed should feel more pressure to volunteer. (*c*) Third, the implication for future favors was manipulated. This manipulation was quite explicit, and its meaning is obvious from the procedure.

The subjects were male undergraduates who were told they had been recruited to take a new personality inventory. After the inventory had been completed the subject received a written plea to help a graduate student. The plea said that any amount of assistance between five minutes and up to four hours would be helpful. Dependence was manipulated within the context of the written plea for help. Some subjects were told that only 10 or 20 student volunteers were needed out of a pool of 700, while other subjects found that 250 to 300 were needed. Presumably dependence, hence threat to freedom, was directly proportional to the number of volunteers needed.

Implication for future threat was manipulated by the experimenter after the subject had read the plea for assistance. Implication subjects were told that the graduate student was conducting a number of experiments and would probably ask for help in several of them in addition to the original assistance requested. No Implication subjects could assume that no further requests would be forthcoming.

TABLE 6
MEAN AMOUNT OF TIME VOLUNTEERED[a]

Choice	No implication		Implication	
	Low dependence (low threat)	High dependence (high threat)	Low dependence (low threat)	High dependence (high threat)
Low choice	4.5	6.5	4.8	5.1
High choice	5.7	4.8	4.2	4.1

[a] The table entries are transformed time scores, based on a square root transformation of the original data.

The third variable, freedom to accept or reject the request, was manipulated early in the procedure. Low Choice subjects were told that five minutes of assistance to the graduate student was mandatory, while assistance was neither characterized as necessary nor even mentioned to the High Choice subjects. Subjects received a reminder of this manipulation later in the procedure.

As shown in Table 6, the amount of time volunteered was less when there was an implication for future assistance. The only other effect was an interaction between choice and dependence. From an inspection of the table, the interaction indicates that dependence reduces the assistance offered only within the High Choice condition, while the opposite trend is apparent under Low Choice.

The main effect for the implication variable has some powerful ramifications. A person who is in need just once will fare better from benefactors than one who requires assistance repeatedly. The similarity to Schwartz' study of bone-marrow donors in Chapter 3 should be evident. Again, it appears as though the strongest plea for help carries the greatest potential for reactance arousal and subsequent refusal.

The main purpose of discussing this study was to illustrate the choice–nochoice manipulation in the context of a social influence paradigm. As the results indicate the threat (dependence) variable operates differently for free and unfree subjects. Only subjects in the High Choice condition should have been subject to reactance, and consistent with this prediction they did show less compliance as the threat increased. That is, their freedom was threatened under high dependence and they reasserted this freedom by volunteering for a relatively short period of time. It is noteworthy that the effect of dependence worked in an opposite manner for Low Choice subjects. This opposite effect would not be predicted by reactance theory, since there should have been approximately zero reactance. However, the backward effect can easily be interpreted as a general tendency to help more when more help is needed, in the absence of reactance forces.

FREEDOM MANIPULATED BY AWARENESS OF AN ATTITUDINAL POSITION

On many issues people are neither aware of two sides nor are they especially interested in the possibility that two opposing positions might exist. A dedicated political zealot may be incapable of understanding that anyone disagrees with him, and the faithful member of an extreme religious sect would not comprehend the idea of questioning God's existence, and even more extreme, Piaget's (1966) youthful subjects do not appear to realize that any of their views are not universally shared. These somewhat narrow-minded, possibly egocentric individuals would have no use for a two-sided communication, and certainly would feel no freedom to be exposed to positions other than their own. As discussed above, these individuals are operating with a truncated version of the attitudinal continuum.

But in contrast, there are numerous and perhaps prevalent instances in which people value the freedom to hear two sides of the issue. Given that someone is aware of the existence of more than one side, and provided the freedom to adopt any possible position is of some importance, reactance will be created when only one side of the issue is presented to him. In fact, the presentation of just one side might well be perceived as an intent to persuade, and as such could result in a boomerang effect. The following experiment by Jones and Brehm (1970) was designed around this theoretical thinking.

Undergraduates of both sexes were subjects in an experiment built around the supposed validation of an aptitude test for lawyers. All subjects were asked to read a summary of a bigamy case and then to answer a number of questions including the degree to which the defendant was innocent or guilty. One of the variables was whether or not subjects were aware that there were two sides to the case, manipulated just before subjects read the case. In the *Aware* condition subjects found that the case was definitely not of the open-and-shut variety, and also that

" . . . the people who had prepared these summaries had had available a complete transcript of the case and that they had been instructed to prepare the summaries as a final presentation to the jury—who would also have seen or heard both prosecution and defense presentations [p. 51]."

Unaware condition subjects were given no reason to think that there might be two sides worthy of consideration. A second variable was one-sided vs. two-sided. The three-page communication given to the subjects consisted primarily of a summary of the prosecution's arguments, and in the one-sided case subjects read only the prosecution's position. In the *two-sided* version a paragraph was included that mentioned some of the defense witnesses and their testimony.

Once the communication had been read, subjects responded to a questionnaire that contained checks on the manipulations and the major dependent variable of innocence or guilt of the defendant.

Since the communication argued toward the "guilty" position, resistance to persuasion should be reflected in ratings toward the "innocent" end of the scale. To summarize the predictions, unaware subjects should not have shown much reactance, for they were only minimally aware of the freedom to take either side of the issue, if they were aware at all. In other words, their freedom of movement did not effectively include both sides of the guilty-innocent issue. Therefore, within the Unaware condition there may have been

TABLE 7

RATING OF INNOCENCE-GUILT[a]

Awareness condition	One-sided	Two-sided
Unaware	7.53	5.39
Aware	6.68	5.95

[a] The higher the mean, the greater is the agreement with the advocated position. Certainty of innocence = 1, certainty of guilt = 9.

some effect for the one- vs. two-sided variable, but reactance should not have played a role. In the Aware condition the effects of one- vs. two-sided, whatever they may be, should also operate, but the one-sided communication should suffer in effectiveness due to reactance. Table 7 bears out these predictions. The interaction was significant, and the one-sided communication was less effective in the Aware condition than in the Unaware condition. As the data indicate, the one-sided communication was generally much more effective than the two-sided, but this effect was reduced substantially in the Aware–One-sided condition.

In summary, if a subject feels free to adopt either of two positions on an issue and receives a one-sided communication, reactance is created and reduces the power of the one-sided communication.

CHAPTER SUMMARY

These two experiments illustrate clearly the role of freedom when reactance is aroused by attempted social influence. The first experiment demonstrates a manipulation of freedom via choice vs. no-choice instructions, a manipulation to become increasingly familiar in successive chapters. The second experiment makes a unique contribution, for the variation in freedom by means of the subject's awareness of two sides (or one side) of the issue is unique, and breaks the ground for a novel approach to defining psychological freedom.

A recurrent problem raised in Chapter 3 concerned the ambiguity of employing only a threat-to-freedom variable in reactance research. To reiterate, an enhanced threat as operationally defined by social pressure does set up forces toward compliance. At the same time reactance forces are set up, although reactance will predominate over compliance only if the freedom in question is important and only if there exists sufficient freedom. The "only if" qualifier is the essence of the ambiguity. It was also noted earlier that this ambiguity could be eliminated simply by varying one of the factors that predispose a person to reactance arousal, such as freedom or importance of freedom. This was accomplished in this chapter, and it is instructive to examine Table 7. The threat (one-sided) communication created an overall compliance effect relative to the low threat (two-sided) communication. Had there been no other manipulations, this manipulation of threat would have told us only that one-sided communications are more effective, and further, reactance theory would have been wrong at face value. However, given the freedom manipulation, the results are entirely consistent with the theory. Certainly the one-sided (high threat) communication does have a generally stronger compliance effect than the two-sided, but when subjects have prior freedom (Aware condition), that threat operates more as a threat and the effectiveness of the one-sided social influence attempt is reduced.

perceived competence ✗

5
IMPORTANCE OF FREEDOM AND SOCIAL INFLUENCE

COMPETENCE AS ONE TYPE OF IMPORTANCE OF FREEDOM

Maintaining an attitudinal position is similar to engaging in a task requiring skill, in that the person is more independent if he understands all aspects of the endeavor. If a person knows every conceivable aspect of the issue at hand and if he has some assurance that his abilities to understand the issue are at least comparable to those of anyone who might assist him in making judgments about the issue, the freedom to hold any position will be important. We may note that this is but one of several ways to define importance of attitudinal freedom.

If an individual were entirely competent and another attempted to influence him, there is good reason to expect reactance arousal. But if the source of influence were more competent than the target, positive social influence could easily result, simply because the person would be dependent on the other for accurate and wise judgments. The following experiment by Wicklund and Brehm (1968) was conducted to investigate these ideas. Specifically, it was expected that the tendency toward negative (boomerang) attitude change would be a function of (a) the amount of threat to freedom engendered by the communication, and (b) the subject's competence.

The experiment was described as an investigation involving a social judgment inventory which was to be given to subjects during the session in two successive parts. For Part I the subjects answered questions about some biographical sketches, then the experimenter pretended to score their responses. For the competence manipulation half the subjects were then told that their social-judgment ability was quite low, while the others were in the high-ability treatment.

The experimenter proceeded with Part II of the test, which consisted of subjects' making several judgments about two job applicants, Al and Paul.

TABLE 8
MEAN ATTITUDE CHANGE

Competence	Control	High threat	Low threat
High Competence	−0.21	−2.37	.07
Low Competence	—	.76	2.14

These judgments were made on a 30-point scale and constituted the dependent measure. Midway through Part II all subjects received a social influence note, ostensibly from another subject. The "low threat" note was worded "Paul is the best advisor," and the "high threat" note said "There is no question about it. Paul is the best advisor." This social influence attempt took place in time between two judgments of Al and Paul, and the dependent measure was the change in attitude toward Al and Paul during that interval.

As indicated in Table 8 there was generally more positive influence among Low Competence subjects than among those in the High Competence condition. There was also a main effect for threat, with High Threat subjects showing more tendency toward negative change than Low Threat subjects. Finally, the threat variable had an effect within the High Competence condition but not within the Low Competence condition. The negative change in the High Competence–High Threat condition (−2.37) was significantly different from a High Competence control condition in which no note was passed (−0.21), indicating a true boomerang effect.

The study makes the conceptual point in a straightforward way. An increase in social pressure to adopt a new judgment arouses reactance only to the degree the subject is highly competent to form his own judgments on the matter.

There is one other issue stemming from this study. Subjects in the High Competence condition knew that the person whose note they read was almost exactly as competent as themselves. This aspect of the procedure raises the question of what would have happened had the note-writer been seen as relatively incompetent. If the relationship between _relative competence_ (i.e., the influencee's competence relative to the influence agent's competence) and reactance is monotonic, then the boomerang effect should have increased, given a completely incompetent source. But there is some reason to think that this monotonic relationship would not hold. The Brehm and Brehm experiment (Chapter 3) showed that a power figure can generate more resistance than a less prestigious individual, and this effect can be attributed to the possibility that someone we have listened to in the past has more power to create felt pressure to change than does someone we have always disregarded. Extending this line of thought to the present study, it might be argued that we never bother to listen or respond to the incompetents, but that the competent communicator catches our attention and brings forth a considerable felt pressure to change. It would follow that for a competent subject, the threatening note from a fellow competent subject would make for a bigger boomerang effect than would a threatening message from someone with no social judgment ability.

DISCREPANCY BETWEEN COMMUNICATOR AND AUDIENCE AS ONE TYPE OF IMPORTANCE OF FREEDOM

The importance of the freedom to agree with an attitudinal position is directly related to the proximity of that position to the person's own opinion (Brehm, 1966). If a communicator recommends to a gourmet that food is one of the central features of life, an important freedom is not threatened, but instead, only the freedom to disagree with oneself. But if the gourmet were told that food is merely an inconvenience, the importance of the freedom threatened would be much higher. Importance of an attitudinal freedom with respect to any given communication can be conceptualized as the discrepancy between the person's attitude and the recommended position, such that the greater the discrepancy, the more important is the freedom threatened.

Three of the experiments in this section directly test the idea that discrepancy between the person's position and the advocated position is a determinant of reactance. The idea seems relatively straightforward, but beginning with the second experiment a new theoretical issue enters to make the question of discrepancy more complex. In fact, aspects of both the second and third experiments seem to disconfirm directly the idea about discrepancy. Because of this complexity all three experiments are presented in sufficient detail so that the issues can be made clear.

The first experiment is by Brehm and Krasin (reported in Brehm, 1966). It is a simple design, involving just a threat variable and a variable of discrepancy between subjects' position and the recommended position. A short time before the actual procedure a measure of opinion was obtained from college girls on 12 issues. A questionnaire was then prepared for each subject based on opinions on the premeasure. This questionnaire was to be represented as another student's questionnaire, and 10 of the 12 items were filled in so that there would be varying degrees of discrepancy between the subject's initial answers and the other student's answers. The other two items were left blank. Specifically, the amount of discrepancy between the subject's initial answers and the "other student's" answers varied between zero and three scale positions on the 10-point scale.

At the beginning of the procedure the experimenter said the purpose was to predict another student's opinions. When the experimenter handed the "other student's" questionnaire to the subject, she noted that items 1–5 and 7–11 had been filled out, and that from these she (the subject) was supposed to estimate the remaining two answers. The subject also expected to fill the questionnaire out again for herself. In the High Threat condition the following remark was added: "We are sure you will be greatly influenced by the opinions stated, and that your answers this time will tend toward those of this student." Finally, the subject completed for the second time the entire 12-item questionnaire, indicating her own opinions.

The results were tabulated on the basis of subjects' attitude-change scores for Items 1–5 and 7–11. The items are broken down in Table 9 according to the size of discrepancy between the subject's and other's opinion. By inspection, it is evident that discrepancy has a different effect depending on the strength of threat. Under High Threat, there tends to be little effect of discrepancy, while under Low Threat, more discrepancy leads to more positive change. If the Low Threat condition may be taken as a baseline, the data indicate that reactance is a function of discrepancy such that more reactance is generated under High Threat when the discrepancy is large.

It appears as though the data support the theoretical prediction. Reactance arousal given a threat to freedom is greater when there are sizable discrepancies between the subject and the position he is pressured to adopt.

The second experiment (Worchel & Brehm, 1970) was also designed to investigate the discrepancy question. Using discrepancies of greater

TABLE 9

MEAN OPINION CHANGE AS A FUNCTION
OF THREAT AND DISCREPANCY

Threat condition	Discrepancy size			
	0	1	2	3
Low threat	−.22	.15	.50	.57
High threat	−.17	.07	.00	−.13

TABLE 10
DIRECTION OF ATTITUDE CHANGE

Threat condition	Positive	None	Negative
Low threat	22	6	5
High threat	20	4	16

magnitude than those of the first experiment, a surprising result emerges. College students were given a mimeographed speech that dealt with the issue of how the communist party should be treated in the United States. There were two forms of the speech: Some subjects read a speech advocating that the communist party should be treated as any other political party within the country, while other subjects read a statement favoring regulation of the communist party by the federal government. Threat was manipulated by loading half of the speeches with comments such as "you cannot believe otherwise" and "you have no choice but to believe this."

Following the speech, subjects filled out a questionnaire containing the relevant issue—whether or not the communist party should be treated as an equal political party. Because subjects had taken a premeasure prior to the experiment a measure of attitude change was possible, and the data were treated in terms of whether subjects moved toward or away from the communication, or showed no change.

Table 10 presents the frequency data disregarding the variable of initial agreement-disagreement. By inspection two effects are apparent. First, there was an overall persuasive effect, and second, that effect was attenuated sharply by the threat. The difference between threat conditions approaches significance.

The distribution of opinion on the premeasure was bimodal, which means that some subjects who received the "equal treatment" communication were initially in agreement with it, while others disagreed. Conversely, some of those who received the "government control" communication were in initial agreement while others were not. For presentation of the data, the specific sides of the issue were disregarded; the data were combined into "initial agreement" versus "initial disagreement." An inspection of Table 11 reveals that virtually all of the negative change occurred among subjects who were

TABLE 11

DIRECTION OF ATTITUDE CHANGE AS A
FUNCTION OF AGREEMENT

Condition	Positive	None	Negative
Initial disagreement			
Low threat	12	2	1
High threat	16	1	3
Initial agreement			
Low threat	10	4	4
High threat	4	3	13

initially in agreement with the communication. Focusing just on subjects who initially agreed, the predominance of negative change under high threat was significantly different from the positive change shown under low threat. Moreover, within the high-threat condition there was a significant difference between initial agreement and disagreement, such that negative change was prominent in the initial-agreement condition while positive change dominated the initial-disagreement condition.

A superficial comparison between the results of the present study and that by Brehm and Krasin reveals an inconsistency. In the Brehm and Krasin study discrepancy between the subject and communicator increased reactance, but the present experiment showed just the opposite effect. Keeping this apparent inconsistency in mind, we should examine the Worchel–Brehm experiment more closely.

It might possibly be argued that the discrepancy effect was mediated by cognitive-balance processes. Assuming the High Threat communicator came across as irritating or biased, subjects initially in agreement with him would have a particularly strong desire to move away from him. However, the communicator was not perceived as differentially biased as a function of the threat variable, suggesting to Worchel and Brehm that they look elsewhere for an explanation.

The authors note that the subject who initially disagrees is in some sense exercising his freedom to disagree at the time of the threat. He may therefore show less reactance than the subject who agrees at the outset, for the latter has not held the position threatened and "may feel it necessary to demonstrate he can hold an opposing position [p. 21]." As Worchel and Brehm note, this analysis raises the question of whether the initial-agreement variable is relevant to reactance arousal or to the manner in which it is reduced. Conceivably the subject who initially disagrees most strongly would experience the most reactance (consistent with the theoretical analysis of the Brehm and Krasin study), but those same subjects would show little attitude change because they have already demonstrated their freedom to maintain the threatened position.

Such an analysis is in accord with the Worchel–Brehm results, but still, their results conflict with those of Brehm and Krasin. One other possible reason exists for the disparity between results.[1] The Brehm and Krasin subjects were told that their opinions on the second measure would tend toward those of the other student. This means that for some issues, subjects were instructed explicitly to move one scale point, for other issues two points, and for other issues three points, depending on the purported position of that other student. Given this aspect of the procedure, it can be said that discrepancy size and degree of threat were confounded. That is, the meaning of the threatening statement was quite different depending on discrepancy size, for when the discrepancy size was small the demand to move toward the other student was not much of a demand, while in the case of larger discrepancy sizes the demand was for considerable movement. Therefore, it is possible that the Brehm and Krasin results would have taken a different form if the threat had the same meaning across different discrepancy levels.

The Worchel and Brehm experiment was free of such a confounding, since subjects were not instructed to move any set number of scale points. The threat in that experiment should have had a constant meaning no matter what the subject's initial position.

Although the discrepancy question is by no means resolved by these first two experiments, there is probably reason (due to confounding) to give less credence to the Brehm and Krasin results. This leads to the conclusion that at least one derivation from the theory may be wrong: Possibly discrepancy operates exactly opposite from what was initially expected.

Toward a Resolution

So far the discrepancy variable has been treated as an entity by itself, and variables correlated with it have been disregarded. But certain of these other variables may help to resolve the issue raised by the previous two experiments. In particular, the exact nature of the information a person has about the issue should be one source of the importance of freedom to agree or disagree with a communicator. To take a typical case, for many years pill-taking women have resisted attempts to keep them from taking birth-control

---

[1] Personal communication from Jack W. Brehm.

pills. These women would not have been aware of any definite dangers associated with the pills, while they would obviously have been aware of the benefits. Given this information base, the importance of the freedom to disagree with someone pro-pill would have been minimal. Recently this information base has changed. Now that women have been apprised of potential dangerous side effects, the importance of the freedom to disagree with an anti-pill advocate has decreased. Comparing two high-pressure anti-pill communications, one prior to this change in information base and one after, the latter would create less reactance. This is simply because a less important freedom is threatened in this age of awareness of dangerous side effects.

In the original theoretical analysis of importance of freedom of attitudes there was perhaps an implicit assumption that people different distances from the communicator had different information about the issue. The further a person is from a communicator, the more "contrary communication" information he might be presumed to have. However, it may well be that this information which was once the original basis of the attitude quickly loses salience for the person. Even though people probably arrive at their attitudes in the first place through exposure to different sources of information, much of that information base may be forgotten unless intermittently refreshed. Therefore, it would be possible that two people of widely divergent opinions actually possess no differential information about the issue, simply because they have forgotten it all.

Imagine two individuals with equal information about an issue, either because of forgetting or because the information is not salient. At the same time, presume that they hold different positions on the issue, due to adoption of those positions long before, when the information was salient. What differential reactance effect should be expected when the two people are confronted with the same high-pressure communicator? There are now two alternative ways to answer this question: (a) If discrepancy per se, disregarding the information base, is a manipulation of importance of freedom, then the person furthest away from the communicator will experience the most reactance. (b) Alternatively, there may be no difference in reactance arousal if it is true that salient differential information is the crucial source of importance of freedom to disagree.

We might presume, with a stretch of the imagination, that the subjects of Worchel and Brehm had only a minimal differential information base. If the second alternative just proposed is correct, then the discrepancy variable in their experiment should not have operated as a manipulation of importance of freedom. More specifically, if the pro-equal-treatment subjects' current information about the issue was not substantially different from that of the anti-equal-treatment subjects, the importance of being able to disagree with an equal-treatment communication would not have differed. Accordingly, it is entirely possible that the "initial agreement" and "initial disagreement" subjects did not differ in reactance arousal. The fact that they differed widely in reactance *effects* (boomerang change) has already been explained, but the point should be reviewed briefly.

Prior demonstration. There was a strong effect for discrepancy in that study, but opposite to what might be expected from the original importance-of-freedom analysis. Subjects initially in agreement with the communicator showed the most reactance. Worchel and Brehm suggested that subjects initially in disagreement were already demonstrating the freedom to disagree, and because of this they had no motivation to demonstrate that they could be different from the communicator. This "prior demonstration" phenomenon may generally occur when initially agreeing and initially disagreeing subjects are compared, and theoretically, the process takes place independent of the importance of freedom.

An Experiment on Importance of Freedom and Prior Demonstration

The previous line of reasoning leads to an experiment by Ferris and Wicklund. The purpose of this study was to use differential salient information as a variation in the importance of freedom to disagree. From the previous reasoning the more information a person has that is consistent with the communication, the less important it will be to disagree with the communicator. And the less important is the freedom to disagree, the less reactance there should be.

The experiment also allows a further exploration of the prior demonstration phenomenon. Independent of the information manipulation, subjects were broken into categories of initial agreement or initial disagreement with the communicator, on the assumption that most of the reactance would be shown among initially agreeing subjects.

College students of both sexes were run in classrooms, and all conditions of the experiment were run within each class. The study was introduced as a simple person-perception paradigm. The experimenter indicated that he would give the subjects successive descriptions of a target person, and that they would be asked to evaluate the target on the basis of these descriptions.

A man of quite high character was described to subjects on a mimeographed form. He was said to have a background in liberal-minded volunteer work and was described as very popular among fellow students. About half of the subjects received additional positive information about the target person. This additional positive information described his work with the American Civil Liberties Union, his involvement in citizens' groups, and his election to local government. The differential information was the manipulation of importance of freedom to disagree. Following this manipulation, subjects indicated their favorability-unfavorability toward the target person on a 20-point scale.

The next form was designated as the persuasive communication. It was described as a previous campaign speech made on his behalf by a political spokesman. The mimeographed "excerpt" of the speech simply propounded the man's virtues. In the Low Threat condition there was no more to the persuasive appeal, but in the High Threat condition the following statement was appended to the communication:

The voters of this state have no real choice in this election, they must
    support him. *You, as college students, obviously have to agree with me.*
Following the communication, subjects filled out an attitude measure identical to that just described.

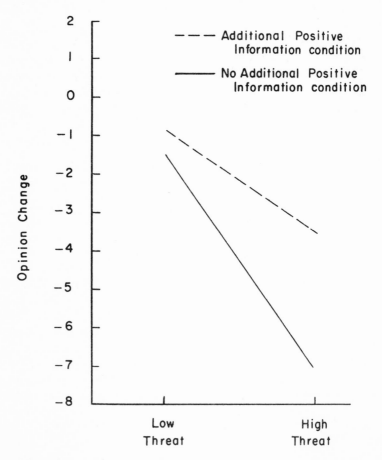

Fig. 1. Effects of threat and importance of freedom.

The dependent measure was change in attitude toward the target person, and as indicated in Figs. 1 and 2 a negative change indicates a change away from the advocated position. First, it might be noted that there is an overall threat effect (see Fig. 1), significant beyond the .0001 level. Figure 1 includes the data appropriate to evaluate the notion that information is a source of importance of freedom. Among subjects given additional positive information, the importance of freedom to disagree with the communicator should have been less. The data are consistent with this idea, in that the greatest threat–no-threat difference is among subjects *not* given additional information, while there is not much threat–no-threat difference among subjects given additional positive information. The interaction depicted in Fig. 1 is significant beyond the .03 level.

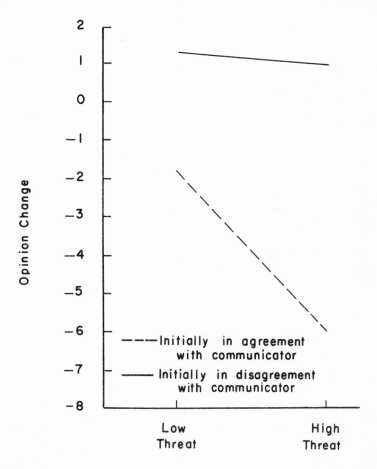

Fig. 2. Effects of threat and initial position.

Before continuing, it is worth noting the check on the manipulation of differential information. Immediately after the manipulation, and before the persuasive communication, subjects' attitudes toward the target were assessed. On this measure there was only a slight tendency for Additional Positive Information subjects to be more favorable toward him, and this tendency did not approach significance. It is interesting that differential information affected reactance processes in the predicted way even though actual scale distance between subject and communicator did not differ between the information conditions. This was surprising, but if anything the lack of difference lends confidence to the argument that it is information, and not subject-communicator discrepancy *per se*, that is the crucial definition of importance of freedom.

The prior demonstration process was examined by breaking the entire sample of subjects at the mid-point of the scale, thereby forming conditions of "initial agreement" and "initial disagreement" with the communicator. Figure 2 suggests that the present experiment replicated the "prior demonstration" effect of Worchel and Brehm. Subjects initially in disagreement were virtually unaffected by the threat manipulation, whereas there is a strong effect among subjects initially in agreement. The interaction, which is the most direct test of this notion, is of borderline significance ($p < .08$).

The Ferris and Wicklund experiment provides some resolution of the quandry introduced by Worchel and Brehm (1970). Apparently, discrepancy taken by itself does not operate as a type of importance of freedom. Instead, the subject's information base appears to be crucial. Of course, in most cases of actual differences in information there will be corresponding differences in position on the dimension of attitude. This did not happen in the Ferris and Wicklund experiment, but typically, information and position would almost have to be correlated.

Importance of freedom is a variable involved in *arousal* of reactance. With respect to the *manifestation* of reactance, it now appears that the prior demonstration effect is worth taking seriously. The last two experiments indicate that reactance is not manifested among subjects who already disagree with the communicator. The reasoning for this is that the person who already disagrees is presently demonstrating his freedom, and even though he may experience reactance when confronted with a threat, his present disagreement seems to be a sufficient demonstration of freedom.

Prior Exercise of Freedom: A Direct Test

The preceding theoretical idea implies that any precommunication expression of an attitude contrary to the communicator's position will mollify the impact of reactance-arousing statements. Such an expression does not have to be defined by the person's holding that contrary attitude. An alternative form of expression might be a verbal statement which the person is coerced to recite. In fact if someone is told to write a short essay supporting the counter-communicator position, that simple behavior, even though nearly devoid of volition, may be sufficient to create the "prior exercise" effect.

An experiment by Snyder and Wicklund took the tack of asking subjects to undertake a prior exercise of an attitudinal position opposite from the forthcoming communication. All subjects initially agreed with the position the communication was to take, and some of them became obligated to write an essay from the opposite point of view. Subsequently either a high- or low-threat communication was delivered, much as in previous studies, with the expectation that the high threat would produce reactance effects primarily among subjects who did not previously write a counter-communicator essay.

College students of both sexes were run in groups and were led to expect several items of information about two men as a part of an impression-formation study. The initial information was about a Mr. Fitz and a Mr. Thomas, and the information was slanted so that subjects would favor Mr. Thomas.[2] The prior exercise variable was introduced just after the initial information. Subjects in the Prior Exercise condition were asked to write a short essay favoring Fitz. (The forthcoming communication was favorable to Thomas.) Subjects in the No Prior Exercise condition wrote on a separate topic and were not requested to comment on Fitz.

Following that manipulation the premeasure was taken, which contained separate measures of subjects' attitudes toward Fitz and Thomas. Fortunately for experimental purposes the prior exercise variable had no significant impact on the premeasure.

Subjects then received the persuasive communication, which praised Thomas as an ideal candidate for a state drug commission. Low Threat subjects read the straight communication, but two statements were appended for High Threat subjects. The first statement was tacked onto the beginning of the communication: "There are several reasons why I think Thomas is the only rational choice." The second statement formed the conclusion of the communication: "There is no question that Adrian Thomas is the man for the job. You have no choice but to agree with me." Immediately after the communication a postmeasure of attitude was taken.

The Fitz and Thomas scales were combined to make a composite score, and the attitude-change scores are shown in Fig. 3. Positive change indicates increased agreement with the communication. It is evident that a threat effect did result among No Prior Exercise subjects ($p < .01$), and that a com-

---

[2]Since it was crucial that all subjects' attitudes be on the same side of the scale initially, any subjects who favored Fitz on the premeasure were deleted.

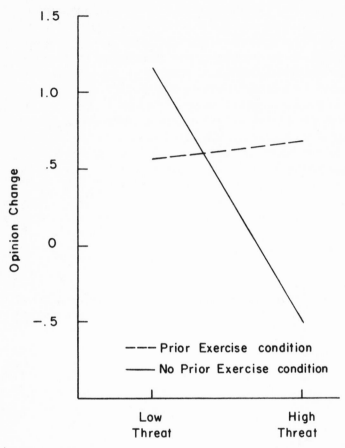

Fig. 3. Prior exercise and threat.

parable effect among Prior Exercise subjects was nonexistent. The interaction was significant ($p < .02$), indicating rather clear support for the hypothesis. In short, the prior exercise seems to have eliminated the usual effect of the High Threat communication.

CHAPTER SUMMARY

This chapter indicates two distinct methods for defining importance of freedom in the context of attitudes: competence, and salient information relevant to the issue. The competence result was found in the Wicklund and Brehm experiment, and the salient information was in a study by Ferris and Wicklund.

Until recently it had been thought that a person's discrepancy from the communicator was a reasonable way to define importance of freedom, but that reasoning seems incorrect at this point. Taken together, the Worchel-Brehm and Ferris-Wicklund experiments suggest that a person who initially agrees with the communicator will demonstrate more reactance than someone who initially disagrees, contrary to the original analysis of importance of freedom and communicator-recipient discrepancy. The fact of reactance showing up most strongly among initial "agreers" is accounted for handily by the concept of "prior exercise of freedom," and the final experiment adds credence to the notion that a person who has experienced, in some way, the opposite side of the issue will be less likely to move toward that side when his freedom to do so is threatened.

6
PROPORTION OF FREEDOM THREATENED AND SOCIAL INFLUENCE

This chapter focuses on another central derivation from reactance theory: The higher the proportion of freedoms threatened, the more reactance is aroused. Suppose that someone possesses three distinct behavioral options and has the freedom to select any one of the three. If one of those options is taken from him 1/3 of his freedoms are deleted and he will experience a degree of reactance. If two options are taken, 2/3 of the freedoms are thereby taken, and more reactance is generated. This obvious method of varying the proportion of freedoms threatened (or usurped) has a less obvious counterpart. If the number of options threatened is always the same, but the size of the original array varies, proportion is again varied. If a man has six alternatives and one is taken, he should experience less reactance than someone who has only two options initially. Stated otherwise, less reactance results if 1/6 of the freedoms are taken than when 1/2 of the freedoms are taken.

The latter definition of proportion is approached in some research on barriers described in Chapter 14. The first definition applies presently in an experiment that varies both the proportion of viable alternatives and the amount of social pressure to choose a particular alternative. Since the general theoretical point about proportion does not require further detail, some background to the experiment can be given.

HIGH-PRESSURE SALESMEN

In the typical laboratory experiment on decision-making the subject has a good deal of knowledge about each alternative prior to his choice, and more important, his familiarity with each alternative is approximately the same prior to any manipulations of social influence, barriers, or self-imposed threat. The present experiment (Wicklund, Slattum, and Solomon, 1970) examines the effects of social influence during the decision-making process, given that the subject is not familiar with some of the alternatives at the time of social influence.

If a man enters a clothing store to buy a coat, he normally expects the freedom to be able to examine and potentially purchase or not purchase any of numerous coats. We might assume for the sake of the example that the coats are hung along a wall of the store, and that the customer can only evaluate the alternatives by looking at each individual coat. Suppose the potential customer begins at one end of the coat rack, fully intending to inspect each of the 100 or so coats. Given that he has just begun this process and is looking at Coat Number 1, the freedom to be able to reject that coat is extremely important, for there is every possibility of his finding something better. If his freedom to reject that coat were threatened, probably by a salesman, there should be considerable reactance. To contrive a mathematical analogy, 99% of his behavioral freedoms would be endangered by the threat. Assume an identical situation to the first, except that the customer is in the process of inspecting the last coat on the rack at the time of the threat to freedom. In this instance the threat is to the freedom to reject the last coat, and at the same time it is a threat to his choosing one of the other 99 alternatives.

At face value, it looks as if there may be identical amounts of reactance aroused in these two examples, for in both cases 99 out of 100 alternatives are potentially ruled out by the threat. However, we should consider what happens during the deliberation, or inspection. As someone picks through 100 items of clothing, he will almost inevitably uncover many that he would never want to see again. In essence, the size of the array shrinks as he makes his way along toward the 100th item. Accordingly, when a threat arises while he is examining the last item, it is not as though his freedom to choose 99 other items is threatened. In any practical sense, perhaps there are only five or ten viable alternatives remaining. Not only that, but his powers of discrimination may be exhausted by that point, and a bit of advice may be welcomed. In contrast, the threat that occurs early clearly threatens the freedom to choose 99 items, because he has not yet seen them and has to retain his freedom to choose any one of them.

What does all of this mean in theoretical terms? The difference between the two examples is a difference in *proportion* of freedoms threatened. In the first instance 99% of the distinct behavioral freedoms are threatened, but in the second a smaller (but unspecifiable) proportion is threatened.

THE EXPERIMENT

The study was similar to the clothing store example. Subjects were asked to examine six alternatives (sunglasses) in sequential order, in such a way that the identity of each successive pair of sunglasses was hidden until it was individually examined. The "customers" were subjected to social influence each time they considered an alternative, and reasoning from the idea of proportion of freedoms threatened, we would expect attempted influence to create the most reactance early in the array.

Female undergraduates were run individually by a female experimenter who claimed to be involved in the advertising efforts of a sunglass company. The experimenter said that a video tape recording of the subject would be made while she wore a pair of sunglasses, all of this for the purpose of local advertising. The subject then learned that she would try each pair on and rate it for the experimenter. Finally she was to choose one of the six pairs to model before the camera.

The experimenter went on to say that the chosen pair could be purchased for half the price if the subject so desired. At this point the *threat manipulation* was introduced. In the High Threat condition the experimenter added the following comment: "If you want to buy a pair, I'll be glad to handle it, since I get a 50 per cent cut off all the orders." In the Low Threat condition she said, "I really don't care whether you buy a pair or not since I don't get anything from it, but I'll be glad to handle the order if you decide to buy them." The purpose of these remarks was to vary the threat value of the social influence to be exerted during the deliberation. This will become clearer once the details of the deliberation period are discussed.

On the desk before the subject were six boxes, each containing a pair of women's sunglasses. The subject was instructed to begin with the box on her right, open it, try on the glasses, and look at them in the mirror. At this point the experimenter introduced her social influence attempt, consisting of the remark, "Those are great." Then the experimenter elicited a verbal rating on a 10-point scale of attractiveness. This procedure continued in an almost identical manner through the inspection of the sunglasses, although the social influence comments were varied slightly.

The purpose of the threat manipulation, which occurred prior to deliberation, was to alter the meaning of the social influence remarks. Given that the experimenter exclaims, "Those were made for you," etc., the subject should have felt more pressure to select them in the High Threat condition, for the High Threat experimenter was in a position to make a profit if the subject decided to buy a pair. The resulting reactance should have led to rejection (low rating) of the alternatives in the High Threat condition. Further, it should be evident that the greatest proportion of freedom is threatened early in deliberation, when the subject has not yet seen the remaining alternatives. We would therefore expect to find an interaction between threat and proportion threatened, such that the effect of threat on reactance arousal is especially strong early in deliberation.

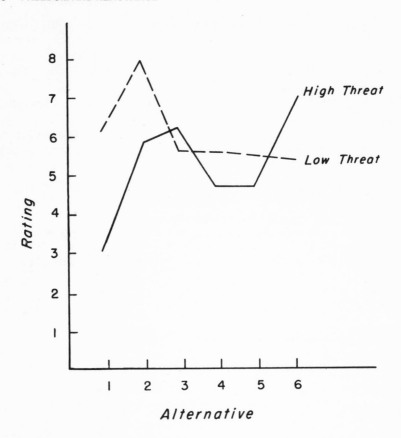

Fig. 4. Mean ratings of individual choice alternatives.

The mean attractiveness ratings in Fig. 4 bear out these predictions. A low mean reflects reactance, and it is apparent that the tendency for greater react-ance as a function of threat gradually lessens toward the end of deliberation. As expected, there was an overall effect of threat independent of sequential effects, and in addition, the interaction between experimental condition and the linear trend over alternatives supports the contention that the threat variable makes more difference early in the array when a high proportion of freedoms is threatened.

PROPORTION VS. NUMBER OF ALTERNATIVES

Before leaving the topic of proportion one interesting side light should be discussed. The second method of defining proportion, noted early in this chapter, consisted of dealing with different sized arrays of alternatives while holding constant the number of alternatives threatened. This means, for example, that if just one pair of sunglasses were deleted from a set, reactance would be less as the size of the original array increased. This is an important theoretical point, because on the basis of one common-sense definition of freedom the opposite would be expected. This common-sense definition equates quantity of freedom with number of alternatives, but reactance theory as originally set forth does not treat freedom this way. Rather than being a quantitative function of number of choice elements, freedom is conceptualized as the strength of the individual's feeling that he can move in at least two directions of his own volition. And operationally, freedom has never been treated in any other than a qualitative, either-or manner. Finally, the chapter on barriers dealing with proportion (Chapter 14) will illustrate the incorrectness of a definition of freedom in terms of number of alternatives.

7
IMPLICATION FOR FUTURE
THREAT AND SOCIAL
INFLUENCE

This short chapter addresses itself to the postulate that reactance increases whenever a threat has implications for future threats. The idea is important in applying the theory to social influence, for one of the major sources of reactance created in a social setting is the frequent implication that the threat will recur.

Take the case of a man who feels the freedom to dispose of his garbage in either of two ways: He can burn it in his front yard or haul it to the dump. One day he elects to burn his rubbish, and during the course of his task a passerby stops to tell him, "You're polluting the neighborhood. Quit burning." In one case the passerby is a man from out of town who will never reappear; in the second case he is a new neighbor. The implication for additional threats is obvious. A new neighbor will lean over the fence and carp at each future burning; the out-of-towner's threat is over for good. Accordingly, the neighbor has a good deal more reactance-arousing potential, and his attempted influence should cause the burning alternative to become especially attractive. The present chapter includes an experiment that parallels this example closely.

While on the topic of implication for future threat, another theoretical point, which has not yet been investigated, should be discussed. This is Brehm's notion that a behavioral freedom that is eliminated can be restored (psychologically at least) by performing an act that would imply freedom to perform the eliminated behavior. If the new neighbor files a court injunction preventing burning of garbage, reactance could lead to the person's performing some behavior even more anti-social or obtrusive than the prior burning. He might poison some dogs or operate a pneumatic hammer in the middle of the night, both of which imply on a scale of anti-social behavior the freedom to burn garbage. It is important to keep in mind that this kind of implication, which is solely a type of restoration, is entirely different from the implication for future threat which is the topic of this chapter.

Sensenig and Brehm (1968) designed the following experiment to test the theory's implication-for-future-threat postulate. Female undergraduates were recruited in pairs and were asked to respond to a 15-item questionnaire containing issues of current interest. Once the questionnaire was completed the experimenter said that they would be asked to write a short essay on five of the issues contained within the questionnaire. Subjects in the Low-implied-threat condition were told that they would be required to write from the same point of view (i.e., support the same position) on just the first issue, and that they were free to select any position on the subsequent four issues. Subjects in the Control and High-implied-threat conditions learned that they would have to support the same side of the issue on all five issues.

The experimenter proceeded to explain to the subjects that just one of them would have decision power over which side of the issues they would take. By an apparently random device he assigned one of them the role of decisionmaker, but in fact, he told both subjects that the *other* subject had been selected to make the decisions. He added that the person choosing would be able to ask the other person for her preference, implying to the subject that she was not totally impotent with respect to decision power.

The threat manipulation was accomplished by means of a note, ostensibly from the other subject. In the Control condition, where threat to freedom was to be minimized, the note considered the possibility that the subject would have a preference of her own: "I'd prefer to agree [disagree] with this if it's all right with you."

In the High-implied-threat and Low-implied-threat conditions the note again supported the subject's original position, but contrary to the Control condition it allowed no room for the subject to disagree with the choice: "I've decided we will both agree [disagree] with this." It will be recalled that subjects in the High-implied-threat condition were told that they would have to write from the same point of view on all five issues, whereas those in the Low-implied-threat condition expected that they would choose individually after the first essay. This means that High-implied-threat subjects had good reason to expect four additional authoritarian, freedom-threatening notes, while other subjects did not. This was the essence of the implication variable.

When the experimenter delivered the appropriate note to the subject, he also gave her a form for writing her essay and a second attitude questionnaire. Change on the crucial item, which was the issue to be addressed in the essay (the question of federal aid to church-run schools), was the dependent measure.

From reactance theory we would expect the least reactance in the Control condition, where there was no threat to the subject's freedom. Her freedom

TABLE 12

MEAN ATTITUDE CHANGE

Control	1.37
Low-implied-threat	-0.27^a
High-implied-threat	-4.17

[a] A negative change means movement away from the position advocated in the note.

was explicitly that of having her preference solicited by the decision-maker, and since this was done there is no reason to expect boomerang change. In the other two conditions this freedom was infringed upon, and negative attitude change should have resulted, especially when there were implications for future threats to freedom.

These expectations are borne out when Table 12 is examined. There is a slight positive change in the Control condition, a minimal negative change in the Low-implied-threat condition, and considerable negative change in the High-implied-threat condition. There were significant differences between the High-implied-threat condition and each of the other conditions.

The results support the contention that threat to freedom by implication, or "anticipatory" reactance, can motivate negative attitude change. It is interesting to note that the effect was quite strong even though the subject was told to adopt the position with which she already agreed. In light of the original theoretical idea concerning importance of attitudinal freedom this may be disturbing, for presumably reactance can be aroused most easily by pressuring the individual to adopt a position with which he disagrees. However, the Worchel-Brehm and Ferris-Wicklund experiments (Chapter 5) indicated that if anything, negative attitude change may be less apparent when there is initial disagreement between subject and communicator. In light of those findings the present result is not at all surprising.

Sensenig and Brehm included two measures that are important to a cognitive-balance interpretation of their experiment. On both the measures of perceived competence of the note-sender and likableness of the note sender there were no appreciable differences among the three conditions. This is one kind of evidence that makes application of balance principles questionable.

8
RESTORATION OF FREEDOM BY DIRECT SOCIAL INTERVENTION AND BY SOCIAL IMPLICATION

Brehm has postulated a number of effects that can result from a threat to freedom, but thus far the focus has been on attitude change and behavior change. A person can also restore a threatened or eliminated behavioral freedom by implication. This is to say that he can carry out a behavior which implies the performance of the threatened behavior, a point mentioned in Chapter 7. Two final methods of restoration are out of the person's hands. One of these may be called "direct intervention of another person," and simply involves another person's directly re-establishing a behavioral freedom for the person whose freedom is threatened. Finally, freedom can be reasserted *indirectly* by "social implication." Typically this method entails another person acting in such a way that would imply that anyone, including the person whose freedom is threatened, is free to perform the act. Suppose that a police officer exceeds his line of duty by telling a group of teenagers to get off the street. Their freedom could be reinstated through social implication if they observed other gangs of teenagers who refused to respond to the threat.

DIRECT SOCIAL INTERVENTION

Two young children are playing with their toys, and each feels the freedom to select freely from among his own playthings. Unexpectedly, the oldest child reaches in front of the youngest and snatches away a toy. Ordinarily this reduction in freedom would arouse reactance, leading to an enhanced attractiveness of the snatched-up toy. However, such reactance can theoretically be reduced if the toy is replaced by an authority figure on the scene. In short, the authority's direct intervention should have the result of minimizing or eliminating any increased attractiveness of the deleted toy. Once it is replaced there is no more reactance.

Perhaps this latter point should not be so obvious. After all, it seems possible that there would be a residual reactance even after the freedom is restored. The best way to address this possibility is to consider a relevant experiment.

An Experiment on Direct Social Intervention

This experiment (Worchel and Brehm, 1971) was designed explicitly for the purpose of examining social intervention. The subject met together with two confederate subjects, and the group was told that it should decide as a unit which of two case histories to work on. In the No Threat condition a questionnaire was given to the subject and confederates just as they began their discussion of the cases. This questionnaire was a measure of relative preference among the case histories and served as the measure of reactance in the other two conditions. The Threat condition was similar, with one exception. At the outset of the group discussion one confederate suddenly proclaimed, "Well, I think it's obvious that we'll work on task A (or B). There's really no question about it!" Thereupon the experimenter intervened, suggesting that some groups have a little trouble getting started. He told them that it would therefore be appropriate to fill out the questionnaires before resuming discussion.

The seemingly uncalled-for remark of the first confederate was designed to threaten the subject's freedom to participate in a fair group discussion. The remark could have threatened the subject's freedom in either of two ways, each of which could have aroused reactance. The first of these is simply pressure exerted on him personally. To the extent that the subject feels pressure to abide by the wishes of the other, reactance should be experienced. Second, if the subject saw the second confederate as being swayed by the first, the majority opinion would be likely to go toward the first confederate's position, and in this way the subject's behavioral freedom would be threatened rather strongly. Independent of the subject's actions, this freedom could be directly restored through the second confederate's annulment of the threat, which was carried out in the Restoration condition as follows.

The Restoration condition was identical to the Threat condition until immediately after the first confederate's remark, at which point the second confederate countered the threat by saying, "Wait a minute. I really haven't made up my mind about the two tasks yet."

What would be expected as a result of the threat to freedom? Since the subject has no direct way to reassert the freedom, the attractiveness of the threatened alternative should be expected to increase. But this increase should be attenuated in the Restoration condition where freedom was directly restored by a social agent.

TABLE 13

SUBJECTS' TASK
PREFERENCE: DIRECT
SOCIAL INTERVENTION EXPERIMENT

Condition	Mean
No threat	17.28^a
Threat	22.30
Restoration	11.97

^{a}A score below 16 represents preference for the task demanded by the threatener, while a score above 16 represents the opposite.

Compared against the No Threat condition as a baseline, Threat condition subjects deserted the position demanded by the first confederate (see Table 13). The effect of the second confederate's restoration of the freedom was to nullify the reactance effect found in the Threat condition. In fact, subjects in the Restoration condition showed some tendency to be positively influenced by the first confederate's comment, given that its threat value had been minimized by the restoration of freedom.

The experiment has demonstrated that subjective effects of reactance can be eliminated through the direct actions of a social agent. Presumably this effect would operate in any of the numerous experiments discussed in this volume. For example, if a person were confronted with a choice and one of the alternatives were deleted, reactance effects would be minimized if someone replaced that alternative.

An important question about direct restoration of freedom has to do with sequential effects and timing. In the present experiment the restoration occurred immediately after the threat. It might be argued that the threat-restoration interval was so brief that reactance had no time to build. This would assume that the motivational state of reactance is less than instantaneous, and that for any given threat there would be parameters specifying the time interval at which reactance would grow to an asymptote. Following this reasoning, it is possible that the restoration in the present study simply served to mollify the threat rather than to reduce an existing state of reactance. The answer to this issue can only be resolved by means of research that would vary the time intervals between threat and restoration. It may be that once reactance is manifested in terms of increased attractiveness of threatened alternatives, a social agent is powerless to reduce that state.

The positive influence power of the first confederate in the Restoration condition is instructive, for this indicates that there were pressures operating toward the adoption of the recommended position. In the Restoration condition those pressures took effect in the absence of reactance, but in the Threat condition reactance was generated in such strength that the positive influence was overpowered and a boomerang effect resulted. The finding of positive social influence when factors leading to reactance are minimized is especially good support for the theory, for it is assumed that felt pressure to change is basic to reactance effects.

RESTORATION BY SOCIAL IMPLICATION

The previous experiment dealt with direct restoration of freedom in that the social agent directly confronted the source of threat. Similar effects should be expected if the social agent simply acted as though everyone were free to perform the behavior, and as if no threat existed. When such actions of a social agent or model serve to minimize a person's reactance the effect is described as due to "social implication." The model acts as though he were free, he does not directly attack the threat to the subject's freedom as in the previous experiment, and as a result the subject sees the implication that he is also free.

If we apply the idea of social implication to the previous study, substituting a social implication for a direct restoration, the procedure would change only in that the second confederate would proceed to deliberate among the alternatives and otherwise exercise his freedom without directly reinstating the subject's freedom. The following study was conducted by Worchel and Brehm (1971) in an effort to determine whether or not reactance is reduced through the implication of another's free actions.

The procedure was very similar to that of Experiment I, the crucial difference being that the decision was an individual matter among the three participants, who were the subject and two confederates as before. The was a No Threat control condition, a Threat condition without a restoration, and a Restoration condition. The threatening remark and the restoration remark were quite similar to those used before, although their impact should have been somewhat different due to the individual nature of the decision. Some detail may be helpful at this point.

In the previous experiment subjects were asked to come to a unitary, group decision. At the outset of their discussion the first confederate insisted that the group work on a particular task. If the subject supposed that Confederate 2 was positively influenced by Confederate 1, the subject's freedom to work on the alternative task was seriously threatened. The majority would rule, and the subject would be forced to go along with the task suggested by the first confederate. However, the subject's freedom to consider the two alternative tasks was restored directly by the second confederate, who told the first confederate to "Wait a minute." Such direct restoration was impossible in this experiment, since each subject was to decide for himself which task to pursue. After the threat took place the second confederate said "Wait a minute" as before, but there is no way that this comment could have restored the subject's freedom directly. This is because the subject's freedom in this experiment was threatened only in the sense of his feeling pressure to adopt the confederate's recommendation. There was no danger of his being dictated to by a majority of two. This means that the "wait a minute" remark could have restored the subject's freedom only in an indirect way, that is, by implication. The second confederate acted freely in the face of a threat from Confederate 1, and this action should have implied to the subject that he, also, was free.

The results are in accord with the analysis and parallel closely those of the previous study. The threat created a boomerang effect away from the position advocated by the first confederate, and when the threat was countered by a restoration, the reactance effect disappeared and was replaced by a positive influence effect (see Table 14).

TABLE 14
SUBJECTS' TASK PREFERENCE:
SOCIAL IMPLICATION EXPERIMENT

Condition	Mean
No threat	15.50^a
Threat	21.92
Restoration	10.33

[a]A score below 16 represents preference for the task demanded by the threatener, while a score above 16 represents the opposite.

The decision in this experiment was an individual matter, and the second confederate could in no sense directly guarantee the subject's freedom through his remark. The "restoration" comment was simply a statement by the confederate of his own freedom, and theoretically, it was this statement that implied to the subject that he too was free. Given this evidence for the theoretical derivation, some general remarks will be made about the restoration of freedom through the actions of others.

QUESTIONS ABOUT SOCIAL RESTORATION

The Role of the Model

The restoration by implication involved a counterattack by a second confederate against the confederate who issued the threat, but from the theoretical view this attack should be unnecessary. For a freedom to be established, re-established, or restored by implication means simply that a second person, a model, acts in such a way that implies the subject's own freedom. Therefore, a model who was not accosted by the same threat as the subject but who acts freely should also restore the subject's freedom. Taking the idea to extreme, a subject whose freedom is threatened may need only think of someone who has chosen freely before, and the reactance may then dissipate.[1] This extreme case may be too extreme. Perhaps the person who acts to restore a freedom must be physically present, and possibly he must be faced with the same threat as the subject. It is also possible that he must attack the threatener as in the experiments. A mere free performance of the various alternative behaviors may be insufficient to establish the subject's freedom by implication.

These questions reflect uncertainties about the idea of freedom by implication. If there were some general way to ascertain when the actions of others, previous actions of oneself, or even states of the environment imply that the individual freedom is not threatened, the questions would soon be answered. Parenthetically, we might note that the idea of implied freedom has thus far been limited to the free behaviors of another person, who in a sense serves as a model for the person. But on a conceptual level there may well be broader classes of events, not always personal, that indirectly inform the person that he is free.

Contrast Effects and Strength of Threat

In the above research on indirect restoration the threat could easily be overcome in the sense that there were no physical barriers to the person's

---

[1]Certainly this reactance dissipation might be effected if he thinks of *himself* as having previously exercised the threatened freedom. The analysis of prior exercise in Chapter 5 attested to this point.

restoration of freedom. Under these circumstances it was shown that a person's reactance is abated when a model in the same situation acts as though he is free. But should the same effect hold when the threat increases in strength? In the early study with toys as alternatives (Weiner, Chapter 3) what would happen if the freedom to play with a specific toy had been *eliminated* while a model proceeded to exercise that freedom? (Such a paradigm assumes that only the subject, not the model, suffers the elimination.) Would the subject's reactance thereby dissipate because the model's behavior implies that the subject is free? This seems unlikely, for even though a person can come to believe that a social influence attempt does not threaten his freedom, an *elimination* is virtually undeniable. In the case of an elimination it is even possible that a contrast effect would result, whereby the subject would infer from the treatment of the model that everyone should be free in the situation, and as a result reactance would be even greater. This is only conjecture, but it does seem clear that the elimination of freedom, rather than threat, is a difficult extension for the notion of restoration of freedom by implication.

9
TWO SPECIAL THEORETICAL ISSUES EXAMINED IN THE CONTEXT OF SOCIAL INFLUENCE

This chapter introduces two new topics, neither of which was an integral part of the original theory. The first of these has to do with the conditions under which reactance will not be manifested and explicates the idea that freedom-restoring actions are often anti-social. Brehm (1966) has already suggested that reactance can often produce "uncivilized" behavior. The second topic delves into simultaneously threatened freedoms. In an earlier chapter simultaneous threats were discussed in the context of some research, but those were threats of the same freedom. The more imposing theoretical question has to do with a possible interplay of reactance created through violation of two different freedoms. With this short introduction the two issues will be taken up in order.

SUPPRESSION OF MANIFESTATIONS OF REACTANCE

In cases of negative social influence there is a considerable potential for mutual hostility and long-lasting animosity. An influence agent attempts to force a behavior or a position of attitude onto another, and to the degree that a response reflects reactance, the influence agent becomes the object of hostility. If there is to be a continued interaction between the source of influence and the target, the target person would do well to keep his reactance under his hat unless he prefers a mutually uncomfortable future interaction. In line with this thinking, Pallak and Heller (1971) have stipulated one of the conditions under which reactance-laden responses will be suppressed.

The experimental paradigm was a simple two-person interaction in which one of the subjects aroused reactance in the other. Pallak and Heller argued that the strength-of-threat vaariable should operate in accord with reactance principles only when expectation for further interaction is minimal, for under those conditions the subject should not be concerned with forthcoming interpersonal conflict. They also suggested that the threat variable should operate in a reverse direction from reactance theory, given a commitment to future interaction, for the following reason. When a source of influence makes a strong demand he will be upset if he finds that his demand is not followed, but given a weak demand (small threat to freedom) he would not be perceived as having a stong investment in influencing anyone. Thus, a subject who is sensitive to such potential conflict arising from his defiance of the influence agent should show more compliance under a strong influence attempt.

The paradigm was sufficiently similar to the previously discussed Sensenig and Brehm experiment (Chapter 7) that details are unnecessary. Subjects were run in pairs and found that they would be asked to write positional essays on five different issues, the first of which was voting age. One of the subjects was to be the deciding partner for all five issues, corresponding to the Sensenig and Brehm "implication" condition. In order to vary commitment, subjects were told that they would be asked to return for three additional sessions: Some of them expected to work with a different partner on those subsequent occasions (Low Commitment), while High Commitment subjects expected the same partner in all four sessions.

Threat was varied in the following way: Each subject found the other was to be the deciding partner, and when the subject received his note from the other (forged by the experimenter) dealing with the first issue, it was worded as follows for the Low and High Threat conditions, respectively:

(Low Threat) I'd prefer to agree [disagree] with this first topic. If that's alright with you, go ahead and write your essay in favor of [against] lowering the voting age.

(High Threat) I've decided that we will both agree [disagree] with this first topic. You must write your essay in favor of [against] lowering the voting age.

After the note was received there was a measure of attitude toward the voting age. Since a premeasure was obtained prior to the study, the data are presented in terms of change scores.

Table 15 shows that the pattern of results is as predicted. Within the Low Commitment condition the tendency toward boomerang attitude change was a positive function of threat, while the opposite trend was found under High Commitment. As would be expected, there was also an interaction.

The apparent suppression of boomerang attitude change under conditions of expected future interaction is an important contribution, in that Brehm's (1966) suggestion regarding hostility seems to be supported directly. Subjects appeared to be sensitive to the potential conflict that could be aroused by exhibiting resistance to the high-pressure demand, and reactance was

TABLE 15

MEAN ATTITUDE CHANGE ON THE
VOTING AGE ISSUE

Threat condition	High commitment	Low commitment
High threat	3.86^a	−5.86
Low threat	.06	1.24

[a] Positive change is toward the position of the deciding partner.

therefore either rechanneled or not exhibited under the circumstances.

This result might be seen as surprising in light of the Sensenig and Brehm results for the implication variable. The High Commitment condition in the Pallak and Heller study could also have been called a "high implication" condition. After all, the subject had reason to expect similar treatment from his partner in the subsequent three interactions. Perhaps the crucial difference between the Pallak and Heller "commitment" and the Sensenig and Brehm "implication" is that the high-implication subject (Sensenig and Brehm) expected definite orders from the deciding partner in the near future, while subjects in the High Commitment condition (Pallak and Heller) had no definite expectations that they would be on the low end of the decision-making hierarchy in the subsequent three sessions. In other words, they did not have a definite expectation of additional freedoms being threatened. But they did expect further interaction with him in one form or other, an expectation sufficient to minimize expression of reactance.

Grabitz-Gniech (1971) employed the record-elimination paradigm of Brehm, Stires, Sensenig and Shaban (reported in a subsequent chapter) with the purpose of establishing some limiting conditions of reactance effects. The general idea is that certain types of personal eliminations will not result in reactance effects. When a person is free to choose among an array of alternatives and one is deleted, increased attractiveness of that alternative should be expected. But when an elimination occurs because the person's peers agree on the elimination, reactance effects will be suppressed, just as the anticipated social interaction of the Pallak and Heller study resulted in suppression. When the group concurs on the elimination of a choice-alternative, there are strong pressures to be cooperative and certainly not to value that which has been rejected by the group's values.

The basic idea was to give the subject a choice among four prints (of paintings), then to eliminate one of those paintings. Just two conditions will be described. In both of these conditions three peers were together with the subject in a group. In the *Without norm-together* condition the print was eliminated from the subject's choice on grounds that it had not been included within the shipment of prints. The *With norm-together* condition was conducted so that peer pressure would be brought into conflict with reactance. The subject was run together with three confederates so that a norm could be established within the group. The experimenter indicated that one of the pictures did not fit stylistically with the other three pictures, and that previous subjects had indicated this. It was stressed that the incompatible picture was not unattractive because of its "unfit," but only that aspects of its style did not fit with the others. The experimenter then asked two of the confederates to indicate which picture they thought was incompatible, then the subject was asked the same question, and finally, the remaining confederate responded.

A reactance effect in this choice-elimination paradigm consists of an increased attractiveness of the threatened or eliminated alternative. The effect was noted only in the *Without norm-together* condition. When the group members indicated their disfavor for the critical alternative, it fell in attractiveness.

These results again demonstrate the effect of pitting social influence forces against reactance. The group's norm against including the critical item apparently suppressed any tendency toward raising the item's attractiveness due to its deletion. Of course other effects could have operated. The subject's competence may have fallen after discovering that three other "subjects" easily agreed on which alternative to omit, and for this reason reactance effects would have been weakened. Further, a possible artifact involved a commitment of the subject to the group's judgment. That is, two confederates agreed to reject the critical item, then the subject was placed in the conformity bind of feeling pressure to agree with them. Assuming that most subjects did agree (these data are not reported), their agreement to reject the alternative should have acted to exclude it as an alternative to be freely chosen or not chosen. But disregarding these last two interpretations, the present experiment plus the Pallak-Heller study indicate two ways in which social pressure can inhibit reactance.

As noted by Brehm (1966), the expression of reactance often requires uncivilized or hostile behavior. Undoubtedly the research already covered, and that to come, has contained many elements of suppression operating against reactance effects. In fact, since the desire to be civilized operates against the expression of reactance it seems surprising that any effects are obtained at all. Probably the strongest liberating factor allowing subjects to express their uncivilized reactance responses is the frequent impossibility of influence agents' monitoring their targets' reactions.

The research in this section is unique among reactance studies because of the conflict created for the subject. Reactance should have been created, since the paradigms were similar to other successful experiments, but the expression of that reactance would have been extremely uncomfortable for subjects. Group solidarity would have been destroyed, and the subject would have suffered the consequences of expressing hostile behavior.

SIMULTANEOUSLY THREATENED FREEDOMS

What should happen when several different freedoms are threatened in short succession? From the original theory there is no good reason to expect any peculiar effects. Each threat should create its own reactance effects, and there is no reason to assume that there would be a summation among them or any other special interactions among the different arousals of reactance.

The present chapter does not deal with the general case of successive threats to different freedoms. Instead, a very special situation is examined in which a freedom is threatened, direct reassertion of that freedom is impossible, and a second freedom is also threatened in the situation. Freedom reassertion on that second dimension is then measured, and the question is this: Will manifestations of reactance due to that second threat be bolstered by the pre-existing reactance? Stated otherwise, if a freedom cannot be directly reinstated, will the reactance "spill over" into subsequent reassertions of freedom, even though those subsequent efforts involve different freedoms from the first?

Perhaps by accident the only experiments of any consequence in this area involve invasion of a person's personal space, and because of this some terms should be defined before going further into the analysis of simultaneous freedoms.

Personal space refers to the territorial rights carried around with individuals, and not to a fixed territory such as a home or village. For example, Katz (1937) has drawn an analogy between personal space and the shell of a snail. The use of "freedom" in the present context should be almost self-evident. Personal space is a personal freedom with the same motivational properties as freedom of definite decision alternatives and freedom of attitude and emotion. The freedom can be wide or narrow in its extent, its scope can vary as a function of circumstances, and the freedom can be more or less important. This discussion will not deal with "intrusions" by inanimate objects, since the whole concept of personal space has been rooted historically in space relative to the invasions of other people.

Examples of the Simultaneous Threat Effect

Suppose a father intrudes on his daughter's personal space by walking into her bedroom, and that this encroachment on her freedom of personal space cannot be reasserted by her directly. After entering her room he proceeds to encroach upon a second freedom by arbitrarily setting a 9 p.m. curfew on her evening activities. When such simultaneous threats take place, it is proposed that there may be an interaction between them such that one threat (walking into her bedroom), on the surface irrelevant to a second freedom (staying out late), actually enhances the effect of the second threat. This means that the girl will react more strongly against the curfew when it is imposed in the context of an intrusion on her valued personal space.

Presume that a man expects to take a 15-minute coffee break every morning and that he has done so for several years. Every morning he has the choice before him, and the importance of choosing the coffee pot is extremely high. One day prior to the coffee break his employer approaches him telling him in no uncertain terms that coffee breaks will be limited to Mondays, Wednesdays, and Fridays from now on, a clear threat to freedom. What results from this threat? For the example assume that the coffee drinker has some means of sneaking out for a break without his boss noticing, so the dependent measure is how many Tuesdays and Thursdays subsequent to the threat continue to be coffee-break days.

Now consider the variable of intrusion on personal space. In one case the employer approached the employee and stopped short at a comfortable social distance of about seven feet, which means that no important personal space was violated. In the second instance he came so close that he almost touched the seated employee, obviously intruding too far. Reactance should be aroused due to the threat to personal space, and naturally we would expect the invaded man to reassert his space. What happens if he can't? It is possible that the reactance accruing from a personal-space invasion would manifest itself in reassertion of the other freedom, i.e., the freedom to drink coffee every day.

This extension of the theory assumes a hydraulic principle in the workings of freedom-restoration. When a freedom cannot be regained directly the motivation resulting from that freedom will push over into a second freedom. It is assumed tentatively that this effect is likely to appear only when that second freedom is in the process of being reasserted. That is, if the second freedom has not been threatened, this process will not take place.

To summarize the conceptual point, it is suggested here that reactance arousals can be stored and can summate if unexpressed. The arousal undoubtedly dissipates with sufficient time, and the present analysis assumes a fairly close proximity between the threats involved. This is why the word "simultaneous" has been used. The threats themselves are not necessarily simultaneous, but the dual arousals of reactance are concurrent. With this tentative theoretical background, two experiments germane to the central idea will be summarized.

Two Experimental Investigations of Simultaneous Threats

Albert and Dabbs (1970) created a situation in which subjects were confronted with a persuasive communication delivered by a speaker who arranged himself at various distances from the subjects. In addition, his qualities were varied so that subjects would think of him as "positive" or "negative." The purpose of this positive-negative manipulation is not important for the present purpose and will not be pursued.

The subject was seated along one side of a table near a corner. Possible backward movement was prevented by a wall behind him and a movie screen to the side. Once the subject was in position the speaker entered and sat down at one of three distances: 1-2 feet, 5-6 feet, or 14-15 feet. The speaker then delivered two persuasive speeches to the subject, one on a public health issue and the other on the value of openness and honesty.

The attitude results were presented in terms of the postmeasures only, with the premeasure used as a covariate. There was a monotonic effect for distance (see Table 16) with persuasion *decreasing* as the speaker moved closer to the subject.

Looking at the results from the standpoint of reactance theory it is not surprising that persuasion was related to the speaker's distance. With reference to the foregoing hydraulic extension, the freedom to decide for one's self is threatened by the communication, and to the extent that a second freedom is

TABLE 16

MEAN ATTITUDE POSTMEASURES ADJUSTED
FOR DIFFERENCES IN PREMEASURE

Speaker's orientation	Speaker's distance		
	Close	Medium	Far
Friendly	39.9[a]	40.8	43.2
Hostile	37.2	40.2	40.7

[a] A high number represents agreement with the communications.

threatened but cannot be reasserted directly, the motivation resulting from that second threat will be manifested in attitude change. Although it would be difficult to specify *a priori* the distance at which an approach constitutes a threat to personal space, we can say with some confidence that if distance is decreased sufficiently there will be a threat. Further, the present extension of the theory would not be concerned (as were Albert and Dabbs) with whether or not the speaker in the Far condition might be inappropriately distant relative to social customs. The important dimension of distance is whether or not there is a freedom-threatening invasion, and at 1–2 feet there appeared to be sufficient invasion so that reactance from the invasion spilled over into attitude change.

Liberman and Wicklund designed an experiment directly from the premise that freedoms on different dimensions interact. The experiment was constructed so that the subject's freedom not to disclose personal information was threatened, and this was done while personal space was grossly infringed upon for some subjects. Since it was impossible for the subject to regain her personal space in the prodecure, it was expected that the severe threat to freedom of personal space would produce a reactance that would show up in the subject's reassertion of freedom not to disclose personal information. In short, when pressed to disclose personal details refusal to comply will be augmented by a simultaneous infringement on the subject's personal space.

The subjects were female undergraduates at the University of Texas. When the subject arrived for the session a male experimenter told her that she would be interviewed by Miss Liberman in order to study some new interviewing techniques. After having made the necessary introductory remarks the experimenter positioned the subject with her back to a corner, and then the interview began. The interviewer positioned herself either one foot (Close condition) or six feet (Far condition) from the subject. Then she proceeded to give the subject instructions for responding to 20 questions. She explained that each question could be answered by "yes," "no," or "I refuse to answer." The latter alternative was justified by explaining that not everybody likes to answer every question.

Then the questioning period began, with the interviewer asking 20 questions. Ten of these were of a personal nature, such as "Do you lie frequently?" and 10 were impersonal, such as "Are you in favor of stronger laws to prevent cruelty to animals?" The two types of items were randomly interspersed with one another. It was assumed that the freedom not to disclose personal information would be more important than the freedom not to disclose impersonal information. Therefore, reactance should have been greater when personal questions were asked, and following this, refusal to answer the questions should have been greater.

TABLE 17

MEAN NUMBER OF ITEMS NOT ANSWERED

Speaker's distance	Personal	Impersonal	Difference
Close condition	1.79	.95	.84
Far condition	.29	.24	.05

The dependent measure was simply the number of refusals to answer
(Table 17). First, it is evident that the refusal rate was much higher in the
Close condition than in the Far condition ($p < .001$), and second, the interaction is in the predicted direction and significant ($p < .05$). In summary,
the hydraulic extension of reactance theory is again supported, this time by a
demonstration that privacy of personal information and personal space interact when both freedoms are threatened.

Summary: Simultaneous Threats

When freedom cannot be reasserted directly will the motivational state
carry over into *any other* area of freedom, or must the second area first be
threatened? In the research examples provided above, the second freedom
(freedom to hold opinions and freedom not to disclose information) was
already threatened, and theoretically these experimental procedures may
have two implications: (*a*) The second freedom must be threatened before it
will absorb the reactance aroused in the initial area, or (*b*) the *most salient*
second freedom will absorb the reactance due to the initial threat, and one
route to making a freedom salient is to threaten it.

There is also a third possibility, although there certainly is no evidence for it at
this point. A threatened freedom that cannot be reinstated directly might carry
over into any other area of freedom, independent of whether or not that
second freedom is presently threatened or even salient. Returning to the
Liberman and Wicklund experiment, suppose there had been a third (but not
threatened) freedom in the situation that could have been exercised. For
example, subjects might have been given a choice between (*a*) having their
rewards for experimental participation randomly assigned to them and (*b*)
choosing one reward from a set of alternative rewards. If reactance had first
been aroused through the intrusion on personal space, subjects may have
been especially interested in having a free choice among rewards for participation.
This possibility must be left as conjecture, for it simply has not been tested.

10
INTRODUCTION TO BARRIERS

OVERVIEW

In the second example of Chapter 1 a young man suddenly became more attracted to a potential date when he found she was unavailable. Reactance theory says his freedom to choose was threatened. As a consequence the boy became increasingly motivated to pursue the popular girl. The purpose of the next few chapters is to examine similar phenomena. The objects lost or threatened are not necessarily members of the opposite sex, but the research and examples fall into the same conceptual categories as the preceding example of dating behavior. A goal object is available, a barrier enters the picture, and the goal becomes more sought after.

In the course of discussing the "barrier-enhancement" effect a number of questions will appear, and just as in the social influence section these questions will be addressed within appropriate theoretical sections. The following chapters will be organized so as to parallel the social influence chapters, although there will be fewer of them because the barrier research has not touched on as many theoretical issues. The following topics will be covered: barrier strength (Chapter 11), freedom and barriers (Chapter 12), importance of freedom and barriers (Chapter 13), proportion of freedom threatened by barriers (Chapter 14), and a special issue—the difference between reactance and frustration (Chapter 15). Toward the end of this chapter several theoretical notions other than reactance theory will be introduced briefly. Each of these has certain parallels to reactance theory and relevance to the research. Further, the research will be helpful in evaluating these several theories as explanations of barrier phenomena and as alternatives to reactance-theory explanations.

INTRODUCTION TO THE CONCEPT OF BARRIER

There are several theories and numerous pieces of research that point to the same general conclusion: *Goals hard to get become more attractive.* This is a gross oversimplification, but it is also a fair summary of the effects reported in subsequent chapters, so the working definition of "barrier" should be consistent with this purpose. A short list of the events treated as barriers includes (a) physical distance, (b) time, (c) physical effort, and (d) monetary loss. There is a common thread running through these diverse events. One could define a barrier as a stimulus tending to prevent goal attáinment. This sounds simple and susceptible enough to operational definition, but the conception also implies several questions.

To begin with, is it always possible to specify the events that will inhibit an organism's approach to a goal? Since the class of events that act as barriers are not listed anywhere, it may be useful to develop procedures that would validate possible barrier-like events as barriers. But one difficulty with validation lies in one of the postulated effects of barriers: Theories such as reactance theory lead us to expect that a barrier will bolster the organism's motivation to obtain the goal. Paradoxically, the very event we would try to validate as an impediment should in fact increase the organism's progress or motivation toward the goal.

Even granting the preceding paradox, the problem of definition is not insurmountable. One possibility is the following. First, a situation should be examined in which reactance (or other processes responsible for barrier-enhancement) should not operate strongly. Returning to the Chapter 1 example, we might take the case of a young man who has no choice among dates; he must take what is given to him. Now, introduce something that *should* act as a barrier to one of these potential, randomly assigned dates. If the "something" decreases the attractiveness of that alternative, we have every reason to label it as a barrier. After all, it appears to inhibit the person's tendency to approach the goal. It should be kept in mind that this first young man had no freedom of choice. In other words, the theoretical conditions for barrier-enhancement were minimal. Now, if the same barrier is tried on a second young man, this person being given freedom of choice, the barrier should tend to *increase* the attractiveness of the girl. Moreover, the greater his freedom, the greater the tendency toward increased attractiveness.

This solution to defining barriers might be made more general. If there is some question about whether or not some event is a barrier, first try it out under the "minimal" theoretical conditions for obtaining barrier-enhancement effects. If the result is a decreased tendency to pursue the goal, then the event is indeed a barrier. Second, in order to test a theory about barrier-enhancement effects, change the theoretical conditions to maximize the possibility of a barrier-enhancement effect, and if enhancement appears, the theory is correct.

The advantage of the above validating procedure can best be seen by comparing it with an alternative procedure. The alternative is somewhat circular and consists of associating some event with a goal object and calling that event a barrier if the goal increases in attractiveness. To revert to the dating example again, it would not be surprising if a potential date became more attractive if the young man found that she intended to take him on an expenses-paid vacation. But there seems to be something wrong with viewing an expenses-paid vacation as a barrier. It sounds too much like a reward. And certainly if a free vacation were subjected to the validating procedure outlined above, it would probably not turn out to be a barrier. Obviously the validating approach is superior to this latter circular approach.

Independent of the validating and circular approaches there is a third way to deal with barrier research called the "intuitive" approach. In most of the research the investigator has simply assumed that distance, physical obstacles, time, or effort are barriers. Perhaps the investigator has assumed implicitly that these events used as barriers would fit the validation procedure, and certainly in most cases there is little reason to think otherwise.

WHAT EFFECTS WILL BE CONSIDERED?

The second delimitation of this discussion has to do with the effects barriers may be expected to create. Because the definition of barrier is broad enough to include virtually any form of stimulus, it is likely that barriers will create hunger, thirst, curiosity, anxiety, and virtually any other state discussed in the psychological literature. The interest here is more focused: Reactance theory implies that a barrier can be a source of threatened freedom, and as such will cause the individual to reassert his freedom. From the theory, a person will become motivated to obtain the goal because of the interference caused by the barrier, and this motivation can be reflected in overt attempts to obtain the item or in the item's increased subjective attractiveness. Moreover, when the freedom to pursue any particular goal is threatened, the freedom *not to pursue* alternative goals is simultaneously threatened. Reassertion of the freedom *not to* possess certain objects takes an obvious form. The individual will avoid and derogate those goal objects forced onto him when other alternatives are blocked by barriers. In short, the "barrier enhancement effect" will also imply derogation of objects not blocked off.

THREE OTHER THEORIES

The following theories each lend themselves easily to interpretation of the barrier effects implied by reactance theory. None is as extensive as the reactance notion, but all of them overlap somewhat with respect to the variables of freedom or importance of freedom. The first two theories, attributable to

Wright and Feather respectively, do not conflict with reactance postulates but are simply less general. Dissonance theory does conflict at one point, that of importance of freedom, and this conflict will be elucidated in detail in Chapter 13. The rationale for introducing these theories is three-fold. Each of them has been a source of barrier research that has direct relevance to the reactance perspective, and credit should be given to them for this reason alone. Second, there are similarities between the three and reactance theory, and the existence of such similarities adds assurance that the reactance-theory postulates have a genuine basis in reality. Finally, there is a point of conflict between the reactance and dissonance theories, and to explicate this conflict will help clarify the precise circumstances for application of either theory.

H.F. Wright: Pressure Theory

Wright's (1937) pressure theory assumes that all psychical systems have a common energy source. A psychical system is an intervening process mediating between certain external stimuli and corresponding goal-directed activities. Presumably there could be as many psychical systems as there are drives, or needs. In fact, his discussion implies that a separate psychical system exists whenever a goal has a psychological significance for the organism, that is, whenever the organism would approach the goal. Wright reasons that goal objects "elicit" energy from psychical systems, which is to say that the organism approaches the goal object. The concept is not entirely different from Freud's notion of object-cathexis. Provided the organism's energy can be directed easily toward a goal object, the energy in the corresponding psychical system dissipates, but if a barrier interferes with the organism's approach to a desired object, the energy becomes blocked — with a resultant increase in pressure in that psychical system. Unless a suitable substitute object presents itself, the pressure resulting from the blocked flow of energy will become manifested in greater tendencies to approach the original object. These tendencies can be either subjective, such as statements of desire, or behavioral. The theory evidently implies the same type of barrier effect as reactance theory.

This comparatively elegant theory stipulates one important variable as an antecedent of the barrier effect. Within Wright's pressure analysis it is presumed that the more valence an object has (i.e., the more attractive to the person it is), the greater is the energy investment in it. Therefore, if there is a barrier to approaching a highly attractive goal and the relevant energy cannot dissipate, there will be a relatively great amount of energy blockage. And the more energy blockage, the more the object's attractiveness will increase.

This implication is one approach to importance of freedom as defined by reactance theory. There are numerous routes to defining importance of freedom, and certainly one of these is through the valence of the goal objects in question. The point is that Wright's use of valence parallels Brehm's use of importance of freedom, although valence is a concept of narrower scope.

Wright's theory has another postulate, which, if anything, weakens the theory. He allows for the possibility that the energy will displace itself from the blocked object to a substitute, and that the likelihood of such displacement will be a function of the similarity between the two alternative goals. Displacement should be strongest when the barrier is insurmountable and is most probable when the second goal can be substituted readily for the first. It follows that a barrier is most likely to enhance the attractiveness of a goal object when there are no similar substitutes available. There is an ambiguity resulting from this notion of substitution. Given that a moderately attractive choice-alternative is available to a person, pressure theory seems to predict both increased and decreased attractiveness as a result of placement of a barrier before the initial goal. This is because the barrier should enhance the original goal's positive valence in direct proportion to its barrier strength, but at the same time the likelihood of the person's shifting his approach to a substitute object increases as the barrier gains strength and pressure builds. The ambiguity may not be debilitating, for certainly Wright's theory at face value does presume that barriers will generally enhance the valence of goal objects. There is ambiguity only because the displacement clause serves as a ready excuse in case the theory fails to predict well.

Feather: Achievement Orientation

Feather (1959a) proposed a theory under the title "Subjective probability and decision under uncertainty" and explicitly stated some of the conditions under which reduced probability of attainment will enhance the valence of a decision alternative. This theory finds its origins in the ideas of Lewin.

Incorporated in Lewin's (1943) analysis of aspiration-level behavior is an assumption that the positive valence of future success decreases as the subjective probability of success increases, which means that success at an endeavor will be attractive to a person to the extent that success seems unlikely. Lewin does not refer to the valence of the goal object *per se,* but instead to the valence of success independent of the object's qualities. Feather has liberalized Lewin's comments on valence by including both *valence of success* and valence of *specific goal objects* within his theoretical structure.

Feather's central assumption is that goal attractiveness (and the attractiveness of success *per se*) is an inverse function of probability of success. He proposes a learning-theory source for this general principle. Presumably in Western culture there is a premium on objects not easy to obtain. Striving after difficult goal objects is commonly rewarded, while the pursuit of easily obtained objects is less often rewarded; as a result of these training experiences the individual develops a general tendency to value the attainment of the hard-to-get.

Ego-related vs. chance-related. The learning-theory argument is extended to two additional propositions, the first of which is discussed here. Feather assumes that the relationship between barrier strength (i.e., hard-to-getness) and attainment attractiveness will be increasingly strong to the extent that the person pursues his goal in an "ego-related" rather than a "chance-related" situation. "Ego-related" means that success in the situation can be ascribed by the person to his own efforts and skills, whereas "chance-related" obviously means that the person's own efforts and skills are irrelevant to whether or not he attains the goal. The development of the tendency to value difficult attainment more under ego-related conditions is, according to Feather, again an outcome of early learning experiences. Presumably the child's parents reward him more for attainment when he has to use his efforts and skills than when the outcome is determined by chance, and through generalization he comes to value those goal objects that can only be attained through personal skills.

The dimension just described has a parallel in reactance theory. The individual operating in an ego-related setting, where success is ascribed to his own efforts and skills, seems "free." Such a person can direct the course of his own behavior, and certainly choices are open to him. By way of contrast, someone in chance-related conditions would not have much freedom to choose one event or object over another. Feather views such a person as subject to the whims of external forces.

The parallel between the two theories exists, but Feather's ego-chance dimension has considerably less breadth than does the freedom-no-freedom dimension. Feather has defined "ego-related" in such a way that success or failure must be possible outcomes of the person's behavior in order for there to be ego-involvement. Freedom, on the other hand, does not require that the free behaviors have any relationship to possible success or failure. Many freedoms are exercised totally out of the realm of success and failure, such as simple choices among consumer items or between alternative ways to spend one's time. In short, there are many "free" circumstances that do not carry Feather's "ego-involvement."

Achievement-oriented vs. relaxed. This is another determinant of the barrier effect within Feather's framework. To the extent that a situation is achievement-oriented, rather than relaxed, difficulty of attainment will have an exaggerated impact on the attractiveness of the goal. Feather indicates that the existence of achievement orientation depends upon the external pressures to perform well. If a person thinks he is being tested, or if there are any other pressures in the direction of high performance, achievement orientation will thereby be raised.

Once again there is a parallel to reactance theory, this time to the variable of importance of freedom. If a person comes to be particularly achievement-oriented regarding the attainment of some goal state, it could also be said that the freedom to reach that state is of high importance. For example, suppose someone is standing on one side of a raging river and can save some time in his journey by swimming the river rather than continuing until finding a bridge. The swim poses a barrier because of the high probability of being swept away. The prospect of reaching the opposite shore should become more attractive due to this barrier, from the perspectives of both reactance theory and Feather's theory, and this barrier effect can be exaggerated by introducing an increment in achievement orientation. This could be done by introducing some competition or by convincing him that the swim is a test of personal fortitude. But note that the introduction of achievement orientation is also an increment in importance of freedom to reach the opposite bank. The behavioral freedom is not just reaching the bank vs. not reaching the bank, but also present is the freedom to prove or not prove personal fortitude. Since the original choice has taken on added significance, the importance of the freedom thereby increases.

The parallel between the two theories is there, but as was the case with freedom, there is not an equivalence between Brehm's and Feather's concepts. Feather evidently is referring to a limited variety of importance of freedom, for there are numerous methods of altering importance that have little to do with achievement orientation.

Summary. There are some striking parallels between reactance theory and Feather's ideas. In fact Feather's postulates come closer to reactance notions than any other formulation existing, in that the theories overlap in three respects: (a) Barriers are given a similar role within the two theories, (b) ego-involvement has some relation to freedom, and (c) achievement orientation has some relation to importance of freedom. At the same time there are some significant distinctions to be drawn between the two approaches: (a) The underlying motivational process of reactance theory is loss of freedom, whereas Feather analyzes the impact of barriers in terms of learning-theory principles. (b) Feather's theory addresses itself only to barriers and not directly to social influence or other kinds of threats implied by reactance theory. (c) Although counterparts to "freedom" and "importance of freedom" can be found in Feather's theory, those counterparts are limited in scope, as shown above. (d) Reactance theory stipulates additional variables which do not appear to have counterparts within Feather's framework.

Festinger: Cognitive Dissonance Theory

The central idea to the theory is one of cognitive balance, and in this respect dissonance theory shares a common motivational basis with numerous other theories. Cognitive dissonance is aroused whenever the person holds one element of knowledge, a cognition, that implies the opposite of another cognition. This was the starting point of the original theory by Festinger, and as such, it sounds much like a theory about contradiction. When a person is aware of contradictory knowledge he will experience dissonance. Dissonance arousal is a function of the ratio of dissonant elements to the total number of relevant elements (total = dissonant + consonant elements) —a difficult but useful concept.

The problem with this notion of the ratio is that some cognitions must be classified as dissonant while others are said to be consonant. But how can some cognitions be dissonant and others consonant when all of them are involved in a dissonant relationship? This problem can be solved by using Festinger's notion of "least resistant to change." When a case of dissonance arousal is examined, it is important first to divide the relevant cognitions into two categories such that one category implies the opposite of the other. Second, the observer should attempt to determine which of the categories is least resistant to change. There is no simple rule for this assessment, but normally it has been assumed that cognitions with a basis in recent behavior are the most resistant to change. Take the case of a man who is given a choice between a pig and a duck, and the duck is chosen. The cognition we should focus on first for a dissonance analysis is the fact of his having chosen the duck, for that cognition corresponds to the behavioral commitment and should be highly resistant to change. Then, by definition, any cognitions consonant with that immovable cognition are defined by the observer as "consonant," and cognitions implied by the opposite of that cognition are defined as "dissonant." All cognitions corresponding to the virtues of the duck and cognitions based on deficits of the pig will be consonant and will effect dissonance reduction. On the other hand, all cognitions pertaining to desirable qualities of the pig and cognitions about deficits of the duck will be dissonant. With this analysis it is not difficult to understand Festinger's notion that dissonance arousal will be a function of the ratio of dissonant elements to the total number of relevant elements.

In what sense is dissonance theory a theory about barriers? In the example of the man who chooses to buy the duck, it is easy to imagine a dissonant cognition that would be based on a physical barrier. Perhaps the man had to climb a barbed wire fence and wade through mud in order to attain the chosen bird. If so, the knowledge that he encountered this difficulty would be dissonant with his having chosen the duck, and subsequent attempts at dissonance reduction would then be increased. This brings us to the next point.

For the present discussion it will suffice to say that dissonance is reduced in two conceptual ways: by the addition of consonant elements, or by the subtraction of dissonant elements. The man who buys a duck can add consonant elements by exaggerating its virtues, such as its potential contribution to the family, and he can subtract a dissonant element by coming to believe that ducks are cheaper to feed than pigs, dogs, or other pets. That is, any expense is dissonant with the choice, so the dissonant element can be reduced by minimizing the expense. The relevance of dissonance theory to the barrier-enhancement phenomenon now appears obvious. To the extent that a physical barrier is dissonant with the individual's choice, dissonance will be created, and as a result the person will show increased attraction to the goal object. This increased attraction may be called "addition of consonant elements" in conceptual terms.

When the concepts of consonance and dissonance are translated into empirical terms, parallels to reactance theory can be found as in the preceding two theories. The first of these similarities has to do with freedom.

Volition. A variable that has come to be investigated widely since Brehm and Cohen (1962) emphasized its role in the theory is volition. To the extent that a person is forced to accept a given alternative course of action, his knowledge of that necessity provides a cognition consonant with the decision. The knowledge of not having chosen freely is a cognition that is consistent with possessing a particular alternative, and as such, dissonance should be minimal to the extent that the force was undeniable. In essence, the individual who is given a duck rather than being allowed to choose freely has a ready-made justification for possessing it, and following the Brehm and Cohen argument, additional forms of dissonance reduction should not be necessary when the goal object is forced upon the individual.

In summary, to obtain a substantial goal-enhancement effect from the introduction of a barrier, a dissonance theorist would place the person in a situation in which a barrier would have to be overcome in order to obtain the goal object, and further, the individual's volition should be maximized. Once the person has chosen, he will come to reduce dissonance, and the theory predicts that one of these modes of dissonance reduction will consist of his exaggerating the desirability of the chosen goal object.

Attractiveness of alternatives. Dissonance is created to the degree that the man had no justification for pursuing the duck. Stated conceptually, dissonance results when there are not many cognitions that are consonant with the decision to acquire the duck. Certainly one consonant cognition would be the attractiveness of the duck itself. If this bird were particularly valuable, or if the man had an unusually strong need for it, the desirability of the duck would go a long way toward providing justification for the decision. The more that ready-made justifications exist, the less dissonance, and it follows that the man will reduce dissonance less if his goal object is highly attractive. Apparently the effect of the barrier on attractiveness will be less to the degree that the goal object is initially attractive.

The reactance analysis of goal attractiveness was spelled out in the discussion of Wright's theory, and it was noted that Wright's pressure theory was consistent with the reactance analysis: The impact of a barrier on enhanced attractiveness will be greater as the blocked or threatened goal becomes more attractive. Here the theoretical complexity begins. Dissonance theory and the reactance analysis have directly opposing implications. This theoretical clash will be considered in detail in Chapter 13 with the assistance of some research evidence.

CHAPTER SUMMARY

A barrier has been defined as any event impeding an organism's progress or potential progress toward a goal. Barriers as threats to freedom are to be discriminated from social influence attempts as threats in one major respect: Social influence operates as a threat to freedom because of the pressures toward compliance set up by the perceived intentions of another person. In contrast, barriers create their impact because they directly inhibit the person's locomotion or anticipated locomotion toward a goal state.

All of the theoretical variables discussed in Chapters 3-9 apply here although the next few chapters will number fewer than the social influence chapters because fewer theoretical factors have been explored in the realm of barriers. At various points throughout the subsequent chapters the three theories just reviewed will resurface. In some cases they apply to the data as well as reactance theory, and in other cases the research says something definitive about their breadth of applicability or correctness.

11
BARRIER STRENGTH

This chapter is analogous to Chapter 3. Strength of barrier is the primary concern here, and research incorporating other factors is explored in subsequent chapters.

In the social-influence section it became clear that social influence can easily have a compliance effect to the degree that reactance-enhancing factors are absent. It was repeatedly found that if freedom was not present, or if the importance of that freedom was low, social influence was especially likely to produce compliance rather than resistance or a boomerang effect. There is an exact parallel in the case of barriers. If reactance-arousing factors (such as freedom) are weak or nonexistent, there is very good theoretical reason to think that a barrier will actually cause a decrement in the attractiveness of the object it blocks or threatens. Some of this "very good theoretical reason" should be summarized briefly.

Adams (1931) indicates that the "law of parsimony" is a general principle whereby a person will adopt the easiest route to a goal once the goal is selected. This means, of course, that goal objects subject to barriers will tend not to be chosen. Another early statement of an effect working against the enhancement process is by Filer (1952), who has proposed that nonattainment of a goal will tend to be accompanied by decreased attractiveness of that goal object. Conversely, attainment is said to increase the attractiveness of a goal object. Filer supports his contentions with the clinical observation of the "sour grapes" mechanism, which is read by him to mean that the nonattained goal seems less important and valuable than it did when its attainment was possible.

Fishbein (1965) has proposed a model of attitude formation in which attitudes are the end product of beliefs about the object of the attitude. Beliefs are divided conveniently into those that refer to positively and negatively evaluated objects. Once it is known whether or not a person views these objects negatively or positively, it becomes possible to talk about the formation of an attitude toward an object that was initially affectively neutral. It might generally be assumed that barriers, as impediments, are something to be avoided. If avoided, barriers would also be viewed negatively, and if associated with any other object, that object should fall in attractiveness. Therefore, a barrier should result in derogation of barriered objects simply through the association of the two events.

The Fishbein statement can be viewed as a specific version of one of the more pervasive and ambiguous notions in psychology: secondary reinforcement. No matter what stimulus an organism approaches or avoids, the behavior can easily be attributed to a specific imputed history of secondary reinforcement, and the development of attitudes according to Fishbein's scheme is no exception to this rule. This secondary-reinforcement theme should sound familiar, for its operation was assumed early in Chapter 10 when a procedure for validating barriers was outlined. In that discussion it was suggested that an event can best be classified as a barrier if it does have a "Fishbein-like" effect, i.e., if it causes avoidance or derogation of its associated goal object. The crucial point was this: Derogation should result primarily when theoretical conditions leading to reactance effects are lacking.

To recapitulate: In the absence of reactance a barrier can be expected to bring forth derogation of a goal for a variety of reasons including the principle of parsimony, sour grapes, and secondary reinforcement. Aside from whether or not these several explanations are independent of each other, it is important to note that barriers and social pressure are alike in this respect: When factors predisposing the person to reactance arousal are absent, both social pressure and barriers create effects opposite from those implied by reactance theory.

In focusing on the research of this chapter, a possible ambiguity emerges in light of the previous discussion. If a situation contains no variable other than a barrier, should that barrier be expected to increase or decrease the attractiveness of whatever goal is impeded? As in Chapter 3, it makes sense that experiments generated by the impetus of reactance theory, or by Wright's, Feather's, or Festinger's theory, have been designed in such a way that a barrier is likely to increase goal attractiveness. In short, most of the evidence cited here is consistent with the theory because a high degree of freedom and/or importance of freedom has been built into the experimental designs.

The following research is broken into empirical categories, as in Chapter 3, in order to convey an idea of the diverse types of barriers and situations used.

EXPERIMENTAL RESEARCH

Distance and Effort

Wright (1937) published a series of experiments stemming from his pressure theory, and a small portion of those are summarized here to indicate the flavor of his approach to barriers.

One of his studies used female college students who worked in a university cafeteria as waitresses. Their duty while the experiment was being run was to serve desserts to students in the cafeteria. Desserts had to be taken by the waitresses from a serving table, and the experimenter had control over the serving table such that the desserts could be arranged on the table at various distances from the waitresses. These experimental distances varied between 2 and 32 inches. Wright found a curvilinear effect, such that desserts located at a moderate distance were preferred over those extremely close and extremely far. In short, there is a reactance effect when distance is increased up to a moderate level, but beyond that, the distant desserts are avoided.

This experiment points out a useful distinction among dependent measures. There are physical limitations to behavioral measures, limitations which don't apply to attractiveness or "subjective" measures. With a behavioral measure, reactance effects are often ruled out due to the physical constraints of the situation, and this could easily have been the cause of Wright's curvilinear effect. Such behavioral measures are not common in the research to be discussed, and perhaps this is one reason. Wright's curvilinear effect should not necessarily be excused on this basis. The results are less than totally convincing evidence, but they do suggest that barrier effects can be found with behavioral measures as long as the barrier is not of too great a magnitude.

A more pessimistic conclusion that might be drawn is that reactance theory is incorrect when barriers become too overwhelming. However, this would be premature in light of the studies on "frustration" to be summarized shortly.

In another experiment conducted with kindergarten children, Wright placed two candies on a table and asked the subject to select one for himself. One of the candies was more distant than the other, and in addition it had a wire sieve over it. In other words, distance as a barrier was supplemented by the effort required to remove the cover over the candy. Consistent with the idea that the barrier threatens freedom, 9 of the 11 subjects chose the distant (and covered) candy.

These first two experiments are straightforward illustrations of the main theoretical point. A simple barrier consisting of a distance between the subject and a choice-alternative appears to enhance the attractiveness of that alternative. In fact, under the conditions created by Wright, the more distant alternative seems to be chosen more frequently.

It might be noted briefly that Wright's subjects were not committed to any particular alternative at the time the barrier was introduced. The barriers in both experiments were present well before the subject set out toward a specific goal. This predecisional nature of the experiments is a point worth remembering in the course of the discussion of dissonance theory to follow.

A comment on the design of cognitive-dissonance experiments. The remainder of the effort experiments reported here were conceived within a cognitive-dissonance framwork, and before proceeding, a unique aspect of the designs needs to be emphasized. Dissonance research typically involves the person making a definite commitment to action, and dissonance reduction is measured only after this commitment. The rationale for this procedure was spelled out in the previous chapter. Such a procedure is in sharp contrast with all other research reported here, for it is all "predecisional." "Predecisional" means that the motivational processes are assumed to go on whether or not the person has definitely committed himself, and typically the procedures place the measurement before the subject's commitment to any given choice-alternative. This unique aspect of the dissonance researcher's approach will become central in Chapter 13.

"Effort-justification" experiments. In a classic experiment by Aronson and Mills (1959) female subjects signed up to participate in a sex-discussion group. All subjects were put through an "initiation rite," which was more severe for some subjects than others. Then subjects listened to what they believed to be their future sex-discussion group, and after listening they were asked to evaluate the group. In fact the discussion they heard was a dull prerecorded session among several girls.

Where is the source of dissonance, and how is it to be reduced? The authors argued that dissonance was created between the subject's knowledge that she had suffered through a difficult initiation and the knowledge that she was now exposed to a dull, undesirable sex-discussion group. One way the subject could reduce dissonance would be to remove the dissonant elements, which in this case would amount to reducing the perceived unpleasantness of the group discussion. Consistent with the theory, the group received a higher rating among subjects whose initiation was severe.[1]

The dissonance interpretation is probably the only theoretical one ever given to this experiment, but it should be evident by now that the other three theoretical perspectives (reactance, Wright, Feather) are equally applicable. The imposition of the barrier (severe initiation) should have bolstered the group's attractiveness, just as the distance in Wright's studies motivated subjects to choose distant desserts and candies.

In a conceptually similar experiment Zimbardo (1965) asked subjects to improvise a speech contrary to their beliefs while they received delayed auditory feedback during their remarks. The feedback for some subjects was not especially obtrusive (.01 sec), while for others it was disruptive and

[1]It might be noted that Gerard and Mathewson (1966) replicated this experiment with a slightly different procedure.

irritating (.25 sec). On a post-improvisation measure of attitude toward the issue dealt with, the high effort subjects showed more agreement.

Note that the measure here was opinion change rather than a measure of object attractiveness. Conceptually the two measures are equivalent, the only difference being that opinion change is somewhat less direct. Stated simply, if a person becomes increasingly attracted to a communication or to the position represented in that communication, such attraction should be reflected in agreement with the point of view expressed. This measure has been used in several other dissonance-inspired effort-justification experiments, including Cohen (1959), Linder, Cooper, and Wicklund (1968), Linder and Worchel (1970), Shaffer and Hendrick (1971), and Wicklund, Cooper, and Linder (1967).

"Insufficient justification" experiments. The research on effort expenditure fit neatly into the barrier paradigm because physical strain is so obviously a barrier. Perhaps less obvious is that the research on insufficient justification constitutes barrier research as well. In this type of research a subject is asked to perform an unpleasant task under varied conditions of incentive. The amount of money promised for his compliance is sometimes varied, sometimes the innate value and importance of the task are varied, and in general an entity that the experimenters would call an "incentive variable" is manipulated. "Incentive" means something that would ordinarily increase the probability of the individual's engaging in the behavior should it be offered to him prior to his performance. It is commonly found that the individual who performs a disagreeable task for a relatively low incentive will come to provide his own justifications, these justifications often amounting to increased liking for the activity performed or increased agreement with a position defended.

It is incentive, not reward, that the dissonance researchers examine in the insufficient-justification research. Reward would constitute presentation of a justification for performance after the subject's commitment, and it has been found that such an approach does not lead to dissonance-reduction effects. The subject must be aware of the justification prior to his commitment in order for it to have dissonance effects.

Does insufficient justification constitute a barrier? If a person must invest time and trouble in order to attain a goal, and the time and trouble are held constant, any deficiencies in incentive for his work should operate toward keeping him out of the situation. Insufficient justifications set up psychological forces against the individual's pursuit of the goal, and to the extent that these forces prevail we can say that barriers to goal attainment exist. If a professor is accustomed to receiving $100 per lecture, a barrier to lecturing is created when the payment is reduced to $50. This kind of barrier should have the same impact as if he were paid the usual $100, but then were charged a lecture tax of $50. The only difference is that the insufficient-justification type of barrier consists of a *deficit* in some valued entity, whereas the barriers we are accustomed to thus far are generated by *inflicting* something (pain, cost, effort) on the subject. To illustrate how this reasoning operates in an experiment, a classic experiment by Cohen (in Brehm & Cohen, 1962) will be reviewed quickly.

Undergraduate males at Yale University were asked to write essays favoring the local police. As it happened, the subjects detested the local police, so there should have been considerable dissonance created between their opinions and their actions. The experimental conditions were created by offering subjects different levels of incentive for writing the counter-attitudinal essays. The amount was varied over four levels, between 50 cents and 10 dollars. After the subject had written his essay he was asked to reply to an opinion measure, which of course measured his opinion of the local police. Consistent with dissonance theory, the subjects who were offered the least amount of money showed the most favorable opinions of the police.

The evidence appears to support equally well all of the theoretical ideas of this chapter. To elaborate on this point, this is a good place to note the necessary preconditions for these barrier effects.

The link between two research paradigms. In all of these theoretical statements, except for Wright, there is an explicit requirement that the person feel free regarding the barriered activity. Without such freedom, or volition, the barriers should not have their intended effect. This freedom was present in Wright's research, where subjects were asked to choose freely. And although the details of the cognitive-dissonance studies were not given here, researchers who test dissonance theory do attempt to build in a good deal of volition prior to commitment. For example, subjects in the Wicklund et al. (1967) study were given an explicit choice not to continue the study. This means that the barriered activity was freely chosen.

More generally, dissonance researchers assume an element of volition concerning continued participation in the study. In the "forced compliance" paradigm the subject is said to have a choice. He can either leave the experiment or continue in a situation containing various degrees of effort or insufficient justification. The greater the feeling of choice, the more dissonance will exist when the barriered alternative is chosen. Conceptually, this kind of choice situation does not differ from that of Wright's, when children were asked to choose between two toys. When a person has a choice and one of the choice objects is difficult to attain or achieve due to a barrier (effort or inadequate monetary compensation), that object should become more attractive. This reasoning is the tie between the dissonance forced-compliance paradigm and the paradigms of the several other theorists discussed here. The only difference of import between the two paradigms is the pre- vs. post-decisional distinction, which will receive elaboration in Chapter 13.

Frustration

Historically "frustration" has stood for the blocking of goal-oriented activity. Numerous variations on that definition and many effects of frustration have been postulated (Lawson, 1965), but for the present, frustration as a complete blocking will be treated as a usurpation of freedom. The previous examples of barriers dealt with events (e.g., effort expenditure) that did not totally prevent progress toward the goal state. Elimination of progress or potential progress is a frequent source of limitation of freedom, and two examples will be given in this chapter.

Theoretically there are no surprises in this research. A person chooses to perform an activity, and subsequently that activity becomes impossible *or* the goal in question becomes unattainable.

In an experiment by Mischel and Masters (1966) a number of subjects were shown an entertaining movie, and at an exciting point it was interrupted due to projector failure. The main variable, the probability that the movie would be resumed, was varied over three levels: 1.0, .5, and 0. The projector failure was said to be an electrical problem, and the probabilities were varied by a confederate, posing as an electrician, explaining to the subjects the likelihood of his successfully making the repair. Shortly after the movie was interrupted a questionnaire was administered which measured subjects' rated value of the movie, the measure including a monetary-worth estimate. A comparison of value ratings prior to the start of the movie with ratings given just after the interruption showed a significant increase in the case where the movie would definitely not be resumed, while the other two conditions (probability of resumption $= .5$, 1.0) showed no significant increase and were reliably less than the $p = 0$ condition. Thus when the barrier was not surmountable the subjects' attractiveness ratings of the movie increased.

One of two experiments performed by Knott, Nunnally, and Duchnowski (1967) will be discussed with extra detail in order to demonstrate the unique nature of their dependent measures. This experiment stands as an important contribution due to their deviation from the usual measure of motivation to attain a goal.

The subjects were grade-school children who played the following "fishing" game. The subject held in his hand a "fishing pole," an electromagnetic device for scooping containers off the floor. Instead of a hook on the end of the string there was a small electromagnet. A cord ran from the electromagnet, through the pole, and to a power source concealed from the subject and controlled by the experimenter.

First the experimenter placed 10 small boxes on the floor such that the subject was separated from the boxes by a screen, or divider. The boxes were arranged in two rows, and in two conditions ("frustration" and "reward" conditions) the experimenter placed a penny in each of the boxes in one row and a dime in each of the boxes in the second row. No money was placed in the boxes in the control condition. All of this placement and nonplacement was observable by the subject. Then, with the aid of the electromagnet, the subject was instructed to pick up the first row of boxes, and subjects in the conditions where the boxes contained pennies were allowed to retain the money. In the next phase of the experiment frustration was manipulated.

The control-condition and reward-condition subjects were allowed to lift all five boxes from the second row over the edge of the screen, and reward-condition subjects obtained their five dimes. In the frustration condition the experimenter consistently turned off the electromagnet as the subject was about to lift the box from the floor; thus it fell to the floor and could not be reached. The subjects were given just two minutes to obtain all of the boxes, and at the end of the time all frustration subjects had failed to lift any dime boxes over the screen.

Immediately after the fishing phase of the study three dependent measures were administered, two of which are reported here. The first of these was a *selective attention* task. By means of a "looking box" the subject could present himself with any of several different visual stimuli, including a picture of a dime. Obviously a relatively lengthy exposure to the dime would indicate that the subject valued the dime. At least this was the argument of the authors. The second measure was a *size estimation* task, which consisted of the subject's selecting a metal slug that appeared to him to be equivalent to a dime in size. The third was a verbal evaluation, but because this final measure was unsuccessful it will be disregarded.

On the selective-attention measure it was found that the frustration condition was significantly higher than the control, but not different from the reward condition. The latter was approximately halfway between the other two (see Table 18). These results tell us that subjects who expect a reward and do not receive it value the reward more so than do the subjects who neither expect nor receive one, but the difference says nothing about frustration *per se*. The evidence for frustration was better on the size-estimation measure. The mean estimated size was greater in the frustration group than in either the reward or control conditions.

CHAPTER SUMMARY

Four points brought out in this chapter can be summarized briefly.

(*1*) The first of these is to note that barriers can be defined quite liberally. Physical distance, physical effort, monetary disadvantage, and frustration all operated as barriers would be expected to operate, given the theoretical ideas proposed here.

(*2*) Effects found within the dissonance paradigm can be subsumed within the "predecisional" theories. But the converse does not hold. Dissonance

TABLE 18

Two Measures of Value of the Dime

Condition	Mean percentage of time spent looking at the dime	Estimation of size[a]
Frustration	50.38	6.29
Reward	33.57	5.10
Control	22.50	4.43

[a]The means for size estimation do not directly represent diameter, that is, the numbers do not stand for size units. The numbers were derived in the following manner. The subject was allowed to choose among several slugs, indicating which he thought to be identical to the dime. If he chose a slug the same size as the dime, he received a score of 1, if he chose the next larger size, he received a score of 2, and so on.

theory cannot explain phenomena such as those found by Wright, because the operation of cognitive dissonance assumes a behavioral commitment. Wright's effects were measured in such a way that the commitment could not have preceded the effect. In fact the commitment (choice of alternative) was his dependent measure. Dissonance theory supposes that the person chooses a difficult course of action, then comes to justify that choice by liking aspects of it.

(3) Barriers can often *lower* the attractiveness of associated goal objects when factors enhancing reactance are minimal. Since it is never obvious *a priori* how strong such factors as freedom must be, none of the research reported here was unambiguous before it was run. Had some of the experiments come out backward, it could have been argued that freedom was not present in sufficient supply or that the freedom in question was trivial. This is to underline the point made in Chapter 3: Unless some other theoretically relevant factor is simultaneously varied, the effects of barriers (or of social influence) cannot be predicted with great accuracy.

(4) Some of these experiments have been instructive in elucidating indirect or nonobvious measures of the barrier effect. In addition to the straightforward measures of overt behavior (Wright) and attractiveness ratings (Aronson and Mills), the dissonance literature has contributed a measure of persuasiveness of communication, Mischel and Masters have contributed a measure of monetary worth of the blocked object, and Knott et al. have in-

troduced selective attention and size estimation as indices of the barrier effect.

The next chapter moves from an emphasis on types of barriers to the theoretical notion of freedom, and as such, parallels Chapter 4.

12
FREEDOM AND BARRIERS

This chapter examines the impact of freedom on the barrier effect, and does so by specifying three empirical definitions of freedom—two of which were introduced in Chapter 4. The first of these is explicit choice, the second involves a skill vs. chance distinction, and the third is the person's awareness of alternative courses of action.

EXPLICIT CHOICE AND PREDECISIONAL ELIMINATION

In two experiments by Hammock and Brehm (1966) some subjects were led to expect a free choice between two objects (candy bars in Experiment I; toys in Experiment II), while other subjects expected to be given an object by the experimenter. Subsequent to that manipulation all subjects were forced to take a particular object from the array.

Theoretically, what does this design mean? In both conditions the subject was given a gift by the assistant without being able to exercise a choice, but in one condition the subject expected no choice. If a person expects no choice there is no freedom; therefore, forcing a gift onto the subject in the "no choice" condition should not have aroused reactance. But in the "choice" condition, reactance should have been created and manifested in derogation of the "gift," and in enhancement of the alternative not received. Relative to the no-choice conditions, this is precisely what subjects in the choice conditions did in both experiments (see Tables 19 and 20). It might also be noted that no-choice subjects derogated alternatives not received, a phenomenon which might have been expected in light of earlier remarks.

Two highly similar experiments by Brehm, Stires, Sensenig, and Shaban (1966) closely parallel the previous studies. During an initial session subjects listened to selections from four records, rated each record, and were told that the record distributing company gave each person who participated in the survey a complimentary record. The experimenter also said he hoped that the shipment of complimentary records would arrive the next morning. A choice

TABLE 19
MEAN ATTRACTION CHANGES OF THE ELIMINATED
AND GIFT CANDY BARS

Condition	Eliminated	Gift	Total reactance effect
No Choice	−.43	0	−.43
Choice	.23	−1.23	1.46

variable was created so that subjects were led to believe either that they could later choose freely among the four records (Choice–Elimination condition) or that they would receive a record randomly (No Choice–Elimination condition). When subjects returned for the second session they learned that the record they had originally ranked third was not included in the shipment, thus it would not be available as a choice alternative. There was also a control condition (Choice–No Elimination) in which the third-ranked record was not restricted.

Table 21 shows the change in rated attractiveness of the critical record. First, it is evident that the barrier (elimination) definitely pulled down the attractiveness of that alternative when choice was absent. However, there was a sizable significant increase when the elimination occurred under choice conditions. It is evident that the Choice-No Elimination condition fell between the other two.

TABLE 20
MEAN ATTRACTION CHANGES OF THE ELIMINATED AND GIFT TOYS

Condition	Eliminated	Gift	Total reactance effect
No Choice	−.94	0	−.94
Choice	−.11	−.86	.75

''hard-to-get'' effects

TABLE 21

MEAN CHANGE IN ATTRACTIVENESS OF
THIRD-RANKED RECORD

Choice —no elimination	.07
Choice—elimination	4.23
No choice—elimination	−5.40

The next study is the final one in the paradigm established by the Brehm et al. (1966) and Hammock and Brehm (1966) research. This experiment was conducted by Wicklund and Ogden, and carries the threat × choice paradigm into the area of interpersonal attraction.

Although there are numerous reasons to think that interpersonal liking will often be stronger among people in close proximity (Berscheid & Walster, 1969), everyone is aware of such phenomena as the "Absence makes the heart grow fonder" and "hard-to-get" effects. The common sense reasoning behind the fonder-from-absence maxim is not obvious, but undoubtedly those who use the hard-to-get ploy possess an implicit understanding of reactance theory.

The absence of a person should operate just as the absence of a record, toy, or movie in the other research on alternative usurpation. Given sufficient prior freedom to choose among different mates, a person should become increasingly attracted to those hard-to-get or even totally unavailable. Conversely, the derogation found in earlier research would probably result from the hard-to-get strategy if the would-be suitor feels no freedom in mate selection. The present experiment was designed to test these ideas. All subjects were shown decision alternatives in the form of potentially attractive members of the opposite sex. Choice among these alternatives was varied, and then some alternatives were either eliminated from consideration or threatened with elimination.

The subjects were female undergraduates who were run individually. At the outset the subject was told that the purpose of the research was to study male characteristics that women find attractive. It was further explained that a sample of women, including the subject, had been asked to come in and rate five men from an introductory psychology class after reading about those men's personality traits.

The experimenter proceeded to say that the subject would meet one of the five men and talk to him following the ratings, then report back with her first impression of him. (In fact the subject never met the man.) To set the stage for the initial attractiveness ratings, the experimenter instructed the subject to look through five questionnaires that supposedly had been completed by the five males in question. These questionnaires asked about various political and social matters, and from the men's responses the subjects were supposed to build a general concept of each person. Before the subject read the questionnaires and rated the men the experimenter added that there would be a second rating, given after the subject had been given opportunity to read the questionnaires more carefully. Then, just before the initial rating, the choice–no-choice manipulation was carried out. In the Choice condition subjects found that they would be allowed to choose one of the five men to talk with later, while No Choice subjects were led to believe that the experimenter would assign them one of the men randomly.

The experimenter then instructed the subject to glance over the questionnaires and make the initial attractiveness ratings, and she excused herself from the cubicle to "make sure all of the men have shown up." Upon returning, the experimenter announced that one of the men would be *absent*, while another would be *late* to the session. To emphasize for the subject which two men these were, the experimenter marked "absent" and "late" next to their identifying letter on the second attractiveness-rating form, which was about to be administered. The attractiveness of the late and absent men was systematically varied so that all levels of initial attractiveness were represented among the late and absent alternatives.

After informing the subject which two men were late and absent, the experimenter instructed her to read the background questionnaires once again and then fill out the second attractiveness rating form.

In summary, subjects either expected to choose or to be randomly assigned to one of the five men. An initial attractiveness measure was then taken of each man (on a 100-point scale), then for each subject one of the men was eliminated from consideration (absent) while a second man was threatened with elimination (late). Finally a second attractiveness measure was taken.

The hypothesis implied that elimination of freedom or threat to freedom would produce a tendency toward increased attractiveness, while the opposite would occur if subjects initially had no choice. The means in Table 22 support these predictions. Given that the man was to be absent (freedom eliminated), there was an increase in his attractiveness in the Choice condition (though the increase was not significant), while a decrease appeared in the No Choice condition. The Choice–No-Choice difference was almost reliable ($p < .07$). A very similar pattern of results emerged when the man was to be late (threat to freedom), and here there was a significant Choice–No-Choice difference ($p < .05$).

TABLE 22
MEAN ATTRACTIVENESS CHANGE SCORES

Condition	Absent	Late
Choice	10.00	8.28
No Choice	−4.56	−6.56

The results are entirely consistent with the theoretical thinking, and similar in form to the outcome of the Brehm et al. (1966) study. The only aspect of the present study that raises a new question is the similarity between the absent and late conditions. When the study was designed it was thought that a threat of elimination would probably produce less reactance than an elimination, but apparently the psychological impact of the two conditions was about equivalent. This may have been because the degree of lateness was not specified, and subjects could have ruled the late man out as well as the absent one.

Explicit Choice in the Dissonance Paradigm

The relevance of the cognitive-dissonance "forced compliance" paradigm to the other research here should be reviewed briefly. In the following cognitive-dissonance experiments some subjects are given a choice regarding whether or not to remain in the experimental situation. For some of them, staying in the situation means receiving a sufficient monetary compensation; for others, there is a barrier to staying, in the form of insufficient compensation. This much is similar to cognitive-dissonance research discussed in the previous chapter. But the present experiments also contain a choice variable, so that some subjects are forced to stay in the situation irrespective of the monetary compensation.

In an experiment by Linder, Cooper, and Jones (1967) subjects were asked to write an essay taking a viewpoint contrary to their own attitudes. Some subjects were offered five times as much money as others ($2.50 vs. 50¢) for writing. Cross-cutting that variable was a choice–no-choice manipulation. No Choice subjects were never given an illusion of freedom, but Free Decision subjects were repeatedly reminded that they did not have to proceed through the experiment.

TABLE 23

MEAN ATTITUDE SCORES

Condition	Incentive	
	50¢	$2.50
No choice	1.66[a]	2.34
Free decision	2.96	1.64

[a] The higher the mean, the more attitude change in the direction of the essay.

The measure was attitude change in the direction of the essay, and if the Free Decision means are examined in Table 23 it is evident that insufficient payment produced the most attitude change. In other terms, the 50¢ payment, which can be conceptualized as a barrier to writing the essay, brought subjects into agreement with the position taken. Within the No Choice condition the barrier reduced agreement with the position taken, and this finding offers a striking parallel to the previous experiments. Apparently barriers have the general effect of lowering the attractiveness of objects under conditions of no pre-existing freedom.

Without going into detail it should be noted that a second experiment by Linder et al. (1967) and one by Sherman (1970) were conceptually similar to this first one, and the results took almost identical form. The general idea seems particularly well-supported.

SKILL VS. CHANCE

Rather than openly giving a person a choice among alternatives, another way to create freedom is to make achievement of a goal contingent upon successful performance. Under these conditions the individual has a personal control over his movement toward or away from the goal, although he does not have total control unless his abilities are completely adequate. Even so, a person with some degree of ability will have more freedom of movement than if his attainment were based on pure chance factors.

Imagine that two people are in a position where they might receive a valued item. For one of them receipt of the item depends on his own skills; for the other, chance factors are the only relevant consideration. A barrier to attainment is then introduced. For example, the person under skill conditions suddenly finds that an extra amount of work will be necessary. Analogously, the chance person finds that the odds of attainment have been decreased. According to the reasoning of this chapter the barrier should enhance the attractiveness of that item only for the skill person, for he is the only one who has any freedom. The person operating in chance circumstances has no freedom that can be limited by the barrier.

Feather's (1959b) experiment is the only available test of these notions. Small candies were presented in pairs to the subjects in such a way that one of the candies was always harder to obtain than the other. This differential difficulty of attainment was the manipulation of barrier strength. The manipulation of freedom involved what Feather labeled "ego-related" vs. "chance-related." For subjects in the "ego-related" situation the barrier was controllable. The subject was required to perform well on a card-sorting task to receive one candy, while a lesser performance was sufficient for the second candy. For subjects to receive the first candy in the "chance-related" situation a high degree of luck was required in drawing marbles from a lottery box, but somewhat less luck was required for the second candy.

The ego-chance variable was cross-cut by an achievement-relaxed variable, which consisted simply of telling some subjects that the task (no matter whether card-sorting or lottery) was a test, while the remaining subjects were told that the task was a game. This particular variable is germane to the next chapter and will not be discussed further here. Once the subject understood what was required to receive each of the two candies, the experimenter asked the following two questions: (1) "Now, if you were to get one of these, which one would you feel most pleased about getting?" (2) "Which one do you wish that you could get the most?" These questions were asked in such a way that the subject gave one answer to the two of them, and his answer was taken to be the measure of *attainment attractiveness.*

The expectations about attainment attractiveness were supported (see Table 24): The more difficult to obtain of the two alternatives was favored more under ego-related conditions than under chance conditions. Apparently, subjects with more freedom showed a greater barrier-enhancement effect.

The results of this experiment are an important contribution to a general conception of freedom. The person whose skills determine whether or not he attains a goal responds to barriers in the same way as someone who is given an explicit choice. In both cases reactance is created due to the introduction of a barrier, and in both cases the barriered object gains in attractiveness.

AWARENESS OF ALTERNATIVES

Whether or not a person is aware of choice alternatives was taken in Chap-

TABLE 24
PERCENTAGE OF CASES IN WHICH THE MOST DIFFICULT TO OBTAIN
CANDY WAS PREFERRED
(ATTAINMENT ATTRACTIVENESS)

Attainment condition	Achievement-oriented	Relaxed
Ego-related	83%	62%
Chance-related	69%	54%

ter 4 to be a possible approach to defining freedom. In the context of the Jones and Brehm experiment some subjects were either not aware, or only minimally aware, that there were two sides to the issue. When confronted with a threatening social influence these subjects did not respond as negatively as subjects who were aware of the two-sidedness of the issue. The following experiment by Wicklund (1970) defines freedom in a similar way.

When the subject arrived he was asked to rate eight men's accessory items (umbrella, cigaret lighter, etc.). Then the experimenter selected two of these items and informed the subject that he could, after the ratings were all completed, choose one of the two to take home. At this point the barrier manipulation was introduced. This consisted of imposing a tax on the lower-rated of the two decision alternatives, and telling the subject that he would have to pay such a fee if he decided to take that item. For simplicity only the two extreme levels of fee will be discussed. In the No Fee condition the subject was told nothing about a fee being attached to any of the items, but in the High Fee condition the experimenter indicated to the subject that if he should decide to choose _____ (whichever decision alternative was lower-ranked initially), he would have to pay a 75¢ North Carolina tax on it. The remainder of the procedure consisted of a 15-minute "rating period," during which time the subject could use an electronic rating device to change his ratings of the items at any time.

The procedure just discussed was for the "Aware" condition, so labeled because subjects were aware of the specific decision alternatives during the 15-minute rating period. Since they were aware of the alternatives, it is obvious that the 75¢ fee should have threatened freedom to choose the lower-rated item. In order to determine what effect the fee would have without reactance entering into the picture, a corresponding set of control conditions was run, labeled "Unaware." The fee manipulation was identical, the difference being that Unaware subjects only knew that the fee was attached to a particular one of the eight items (e.g., the umbrella), but they had no idea that that item was to be a decision alternative.

The main dependent measure was the rating change derived from the initial premanipulation measure and a second measure taken approximately 15 minutes later (but before the choice) as the postmeasure. Table 25 summarizes the change scores for the lower-rated decision alternative. First, it might be noted that the fee does indeed act as a barrier. When reactance is impossible (i.e., in the Unaware condition) the critical item is pulled down considerably by the fee. By way of contrast, there is virtually no rating change for the critical item in the Aware High Fee condition. Apparently the threat to freedom tends to move the item upward in rating, countering the strong forces toward derogation set up by the barrier.

Within the No Fee condition there is some slight tendency for the critical item to *drop* in attractiveness in the Aware condition, and the fee × awareness interaction is significant.

Summary

The results provide support for the proposition that money can act as a barrier and cause a choice object to be more highly evaluated. The results are entirely consistent with the Jones and Brehm finding that awareness of decision alternatives can be effective as a manipulation of freedom.

Much of the dissonance literature already discussed has used differential payment as a dissonance inducer. The findings consistently demonstrated that a person who chooses to perform an act for insufficient payment becomes increasingly attracted to that action, or more in agreement with the

TABLE 25

MEAN RATING CHANGE FOR THE
LOWER-RATED ALTERNATIVE

Level of fee	Aware	Unaware	Difference (reactance effect)
High Fee	.40[a]	−11.47	11.87[b]
No Fee	−1.73	.53	−2.26

[a] A positive mean change indicates increased attractiveness.
[b] A positive difference score indicates a reactance effect.

action. This experiment also used a variable of money, and it was found as in the dissonance research that subjects become attracted to a costly option as long as they initially have freedom of choice. The important point is that this process can occur prior to any overt commitment, as this experiment has shown.

CHAPTER SUMMARY

The point of this chapter has been made consistently in a variety of contexts: pre-existing freedom is a prerequisite for a barrier to have reactance-like effects. The notion has been tested by giving subjects explicit choice, by varying conditions of skill and chance, and by manipulating subjects' awareness of specific alternatives. Further, the effect operates whether or not the subject has already chosen an alternative.

Validation of Barriers

Another idea brought out in this chapter goes back to Chapter 10, in which a validation procedure for barriers was discussed. According to this procedure, an event can be established as a barrier by first observing that it causes derogation under conditions where reactance should not be expected. Once this has been accomplished, that same event can be imposed under conditions where reactance would be expected (such as conditions of free choice). In most of the "no choice" or "unfree" conditions of these experiments there was such a derogation effect, signifying that this chapter was indeed dealing with barriers rather than with non-barrier events that might have led to spurious effects. Such spurious effects, and how to avoid them through this validation procedure, can be seen by re-examining the procedure of the experiment by Wicklund.

Suppose that just the Aware condition had been used and the fee had been the sole variable. Suppose further that the 75¢ fee had created an increased rating relative to the 0 fee. This would appear to be a barrier effect, but the effect would have to be assumed, since the barrier had never been validated. The assumption that a 75¢ fee was a barrier may have been unfounded. For example, a special tax could have implied high quality material, thereby causing an automatic increased rating. In such a case the increase would not be due to a barrier, but instead, to something positive (high quality, or luxury) being associated with the choice object. The purpose of the Unaware condition was to determine what impact the fee has on the object when conditions for reactance arousal are minimal, and as the results indicated, the fee did lower the attractiveness of the object when the subject did not know that the barriered object was to be chosen.

Which Theories Apply?

Some of the limitations of Feather's and Wright's formulations were discussed earlier, and these limitations can be reviewed quickly. Although Wright's notion fit the results of the previous chapter when threat was the only variable, his theory has no formal statement of a variable resembling freedom. For that reason his ideas cannot be applied here. The difficulty with Feather's theory is in its limited concept of freedom. His "ego-involvement" variable fits his own experiment rather well, but that variable seems limited to variations of freedom that carry a dimension of success-failure. Therefore, in most situations of the choice–no-choice nature discussed here, his concept of ego-involvement applies only with a stretch of the imagination. The important point, however, is the parallel between ego-involvement and freedom in general. Certainly ego-involvement is one workable definition of freedom.

How does dissonance theory handle the results? There is no problem about the freedom variable, for that is an intrinsic aspect of the theory. The difficulty in applying dissonance principles to the "non-dissonance" research of this and the previous chapter lies in the requirement that dissonance reduction be measured postdecisionally. There is a good theoretical reason for this postdecisional measurement. In order to know which direction dissonance-reduction processes will take, the relative resistance to change of the relevant cognitions must be assessed or understood. The application of the theory has historically been seen as ambiguous unless resistance to change has been inferred from a behavioral commitment.

Given this background, how would dissonance theory be applied to the Brehm et al. (1966) experiment, for example? First, a dissonance theorist would ask in what way the subject has committed himself. The answer, of course, is that there has been no commitment. Possibly a premature commitment to one of the records could be read into that experiment, but this only magnifies the problem of applying dissonance theory. This is because it was the third-ranked alternative that was subject to a barrier in the Brehm et al. (1966) study, and if there had been a premature commitment, that commitment more than likely would have been to the first-ranked record.

A crucial distinction between cognitive dissonance and reactance theories has now emerged. As should be evident, the application of reactance theory does not assume a commitment of any particular nature. The tests of the theory have been predecisional, in that decision freedom has been threatened before the person has made up his mind.[1] But this does not mean that such effects will fail to be manifested after the commitment has taken place. In all

---

[1]The sole exception to this rule is in Chapter 16, where the theory is extended to postdecision regret.

of the dissonance experiments reported the barrier was introduced prior to the choice point, and it is quite reasonable to think that the barrier effect occurred as soon as the subject was aware of it, and then the effect carried over beyond the commitment.

13
IMPORTANCE OF FREEDOM AND BARRIERS

THREE ADDITIONAL INSTANCES OF IMPORTANCE OF FREEDOM

In Chapter 5 importance of freedom was introduced in the context of threat to opinion freedom. Three operational definitions of importance were investigated there—competence to hold an opinion, communicator-recipient discrepancy, and communication-relevant information possessed by the recipient. More generally, importance of a free behavior (Brehm, 1966) is ". . . a direct function of the unique instrumental value which that behavior has for the satisfaction of needs, multiplied by the actual or potential maximum magnitude of those needs [pp. 4–5]." In the present context of discrete choices and barriers this definition has a number of implications, three of which will be discussed. The existing research with barriers has operationally defined importance of freedom in the following three ways: (a) amount of cognitive overlap between decision alternatives, (b) presence of motives of personal achievement, and (c) attractiveness of alternatives. These three are taken up in order below, and in the course of examining the last, some extended discussion will be given to the theory of cognitive dissonance.

Cognitive Overlap

When there is considerable qualitative overlap between the alternatives available in a decision, importance of freedom to choose one over another is minimal. To take an extreme case, a child might be given a choice between two ice cream cones. They are of the same flavor, size, temperature, and texture, and he is asked to choose between them. Just prior to his choice one of them is removed, and from the previous thinking a reactance effect would be expected. But how great should this effect be? In this instance the behavioral freedom to choose the usurped ice cream cone is of no importance, for that freedom satisfied no unique need. The freedom is a useless one. However, if the cones were to differ in flavor or other respects, the freedom to choose one over another would have some instrumental value. On some occasions a person may want chocolate, and on others vanilla, and for this reason the freedom would be of some importance. Wright's research has been the only relevant investigation of cognitive overlap and barriers.

Three quite similar experiments were conducted with kindergarten children in order to test the effects of an "effort" barrier. In the course of these experiments Wright seems to have discovered the cognitive overlap phenomenon.

The subject was brought into a room and led to a corner where two pieces of candy had been suspended from the ceiling with string. One piece of candy was within the child's grasp, but the other (11 inches higher) could not be reached by the subject except by his standing on a chair. The experimenter indicated that the subject could take either of the candies and keep it.

In the first two experiments the subjects showed a clear preference for the candy easiest to reach. In the first study all 8 of the subjects chose the nearest candy, and in the second study 8 of the 10 subjects did the same. Because these results were disparate with those of the cafeteria experiment (Chapter 11), Wright examined some of the differences between the two sets of research and noted that the choice alternatives were not identical in the cafeteria experiment. Accordingly, in the third string-suspension experiment the two candies differed in color, and the change effected results more in keeping with pressure theory. Ten of the 19 subjects chose the more distant alternative. (See Table 26 for a comparison of the experiments.)

Wright has uncovered an important phenomenon. In a choice situation a barrier will enhance the attractiveness of an alternative only to the extent that the alternatives are not identical. Wright's explanation for this effect is derived from his pressure theory and simply assumes that two identical choice alternatives are functionally equivalent to a single goal. Because of this identity they correspond to the same psychical system. By "correspond to the same psychical system" Wright means that the alternatives satisfy the same need, and because either alternative is appropriate for discharge of the tension, the principle of parsimony comes into play. When the alternatives are not equivalent there is a separate "psychical system" or "need" corresponding to each alternative, and prior to selection of an alternative the pressure corresponding to one of the needs can be built up as a result of the barrier. It is important to note that this increase in pressure is prior to selection of the goal, for once a goal object is chosen the principle of parsimony will lead the person to take the easiest route to obtaining it. When the candies were identical the goal had already been chosen in the sense that the alternatives comprised a single goal; consequently, the principle of parsimony came into effect immediately.

TABLE 26
THE EFFECT OF SIMILARITY OF CHOICE ALTERNATIVES
(STRING-SUSPENSION EXPERIMENTS)

Experiment	Number of subjects choosing each alternative		
	Easy to obtain	Difficult to obtain	N
Experiments I and II Combined (Choice alternatives equivalent)	16	2	18
Experiment III (Choice alternatives different)	9	10	19

Note.—The difference between Experiments I and II combined and Experiment III is significant beyond the .05 level.

There is an analogy between Wright's analysis of similar and dissimilar alternatives and the notion of "cognitive overlap" investigated by Brehm and Cohen (1959) and by Brock (1963). Cognitive overlap means that decision alternatives are similar in numerous attributes. If they are totally similar there is no postdecision dissonance, since nothing is foregone by rejecting an alternative. In other words, the alternatives are part of the same psychical system (Wright), and neither one has an independent psychological significance for the decision-maker.

The reactance-theory analysis of cognitive overlap has already been spelled out, and Wright's series of three studies supports the notion well. Apparently a freedom is unimportant when decision alternatives are identical or nearly so. It should be remembered, however, that nonidentity *per se* is merely a necessary condition for importance of freedom. Nonidentity is not a sufficient condition. It is also required that the nonidentical alternatives carry some discriminable function or instrumental value for the person.

Achievement Orientation

When a person has the freedom to pursue an alternative or not, such freedom can be exaggerated in importance by attaching a value of *personal achievement* to the attainment of the goal. This should be obvious. The more personal needs a behavioral freedom can satisfy, the more important the freedom is. Three experiments have been conducted to test this notion, all inspired by Feather's notion of achievement orientation. As already noted, achievement orientation is one specific form of importance of freedom.

In the previous chapter an experiment by Feather was described which involved a variation in achievement instructions among other variables. To recapitulate, subjects were asked to perform a task involving either skill or chance, if they were to win some candy. Half of the subjects were told that the task was a test (achievement-oriented instructions), while the other half were told it was a game (relaxed instructions). As indicated in Table 24 of Chapter 12, the more difficult-to-obtain candy was especially preferred under achievement-oriented instructions.

Wicklund, Robin, and Robin conducted two experiments in the same vein as Feather's investigation of achievement orientation. In the first of these, achievement orientation was induced by telling some subjects that not too many people are capable of attaining the goal. It was assumed that feelings of achievement orientation would be created, given that goal attainment was a challenge. In the second experiment a manipulation more in line with Feather's was used.

In the first experiment, male subjects were recruited in groups of four and were seated in a room where they were separated visually by dividers. The experimenter said that they were to take an I.Q. test consisting of fitting blocks together in a pattern. The experimenter demonstrated how the task was to be performed. Achievement orientation was varied by giving subjects feedback concerning the purported performance of their peers on the task: In the High Achievement condition subjects were told that 30% of those who had previously attempted the task completed it successfully in the allotted half hour, whereas in the Low Achievement condition subjects learned that the task was successfully completed by all who had previously attempted it. All subjects were promised a two-dollar gift certificate should they successfully complete the task within the allotted time. At that point a second experimenter took over and manipulated the barrier. Approximately half of the subjects were led to believe that they would have to travel about two miles in order to pick up the gift certificate, if they were successful at the task, and the remainder of the subjects were not informed of any physical effort. Finally a questionnaire was administered that asked the subjects to indicate the dollar value of the gift certificate.

The second experiment differed from the first in two major respects. Achievement orientation was manipulated in terms of the importance of the task, rather than through probability. High Achievement subjects were told that the task was a measure of intelligence, and Low Achievement subjects

TABLE 27
MEAN RATED VALUE OF TWO-DOLLAR GIFT CERTIFICATE
(EXPERIMENT I)

Barrier	High achievement	Low achievement
High physical barrier (distance)	$1.94	$1.67
Low physical barrier (distance)	$1.55	$1.91
Mean difference between high and low barrier	$ .39	$–.24

were led to believe that the test did not measure anything of psychological significance. The barrier was temporal rather than physical: Some subjects learned that they would have to wait three weeks to receive the gift certificate if they earned it, and the others expected no wait. Again, the subjects were asked for a personal estimate of the monetary worth of the gift certificate.

Feather's theory predicts that the estimated monetary worth of the gift certificate should increase as the barrier increases, but only to the extent that achievement orientation is high. Consistent with this prediction there was a positive relationship between barrier strength and estimated value, given high achievement orientation, but just the opposite relationship prevailed under low achievement orientation (see Tables 27 and 28). The statistical interactions were significant in both studies ($p < .025$ and $p < .01$).

TABLE 28
MEAN RATED VALUE OF TWO-DOLLAR GIFT CERTIFICATE
(EXPERIMENT II)

Barrier	High achievement	Low achievement
High temporal barrier (3 weeks)	$1.86	$1.48
Low temporal barrier (no delay)	$1.70	$1.95
Mean difference between high and low barrier	$ .16	$–.47

The results of these experiments are quite similar. All three of them point to the conclusion that barriers have a great impact when importance of freedom is bolstered through the presence of achievement orientation. This means, of course, that the results are also supportive of Feather's notion.

Attractiveness of Alternatives

Importance of a free behavior, as noted earlier, is ". . . a direct function of the unique instrumental value which that behavior has for the satisfaction of needs . . ." Brehm's conception of importance can be applied readily to the attractiveness of alternatives. Almost implicit in the definition is that a threat to an attractive alternative should make for more reactance than a threat to a relatively unattractive option. This is because an alternative sought after by a person is bound to be instrumental in present or future need satisfaction.

Toward the end of Chapter 5, also on importance of freedom, an analogous statement was made about opinion freedom. On the basis of recent research there was a suggestion that a person who has evidence or reason for taking a particular position will experience less reactance when pressured to adopt that position than when pressured to adopt the opposite position. The reason is that holding a position that has substantial support will lead to more successful or adaptive behaviors, at least from the person's point of view. The person who holds a well-supported position can expect that acting on that position, rather than on others, will maximize potential need satisfaction. The analysis of attractiveness of alternatives is very close to the analysis of "attractiveness" of attitudinal positions, and similar experimental results should be expected.

The research of this section consists primarily of two major experiments, preceded with a minor result reported by Wright. An experiment by Worchel then addresses itself directly to the attractiveness issue. Extra detail is given to this experiment, since in this volume it is the only one reported that uses hostility or aggression as a manifestation of reactance. Finally an experiment by Aronson in the dissonance tradition underlines the major conflict between reactance and dissonance theories as applied to barriers. Some attention is then given toward a resolution of the conflict.

Wright. The first available evidence on this point is from Wright's cafeteria study, summarized at the beginning of Chapter 11. An aspect not discussed was Wright's measurement of the valence of the desserts. Consistent with both his theory and the present ideas, he found the enhancement effect of the barrier to be greater for desserts of high attractiveness. Unfortunately, there is a serious disqualifier associated with Wright's conclusion—he presents no statistical evidence for this point. But at least there is a hint of evidence in the direction that would be expected, and with this lead-in Worchel's more definitive study can be examined.

TABLE 29

MEAN HOSTILITY SCORES
UNDER CHOICE CONDITIONS[a]

Attractiveness of alternative received		
Most attractive	Second most attractive	Least attractive
13.57	17.07	22.21

[a] A high number represents high hostility.

Worchel. Worchel's (1971) study of reactance and frustration will be taken up in detail in Chapter 15. For the theoretical question of interest here, just a portion of it need be discussed. Male undergraduates were told that the effects of different kinds of incentives on task performance were being studied. They found that they would be asked to perform two tasks, and subjects in the Choice condition[1] were led to expect to choose their form of compensation from three types of prizes: an hour's worth of experimental credit, five dollars, or men's cologne.

Subsequently, a second experimenter violated the subject's freedom by assigning him an alternative. Based on the subject's earlier ratings of the three alternative prizes he was assigned either the most attractive, second most attractive, or least attractive alternative. Then measures of hostility toward the second experimenter were taken.

Brehm (1966) has indicated that reactance might well be accompanied by feelings of hostility. If so, such hostility should be a direct function of the importance of freedom threatened, and in the Worchel experiment hostility should be greatest when the subject receives the least attractive alternative. As shown in Table 29, the results are entirely consistent with this reasoning.

Although this experiment directly supports the proposition about attractiveness of alternatives, it does so with a measure of hostility rather than with the more direct measures to which we are accustomed. For this reason it would be useful to look at a similar experiment which incorporates the more traditional measure. Such an experiment is reported in Chapter 16 (Brehm & Rozen, 1971), in which the threat was of the self-imposed variety. The self-imposed issue will be taken up in that chapter, but the important point for

[1] Two other conditions were also run, to be discussed in Chapter 15.

now is that the Brehm and Rozen effects for initial attractiveness were almost identical to those of Worchel, although reactance in their study was measured by change in attractiveness. Therefore, the theoretical point seems to be established. The next experiment, by Aronson, introduces a complication.

Aronson (1961). Subjects were asked to "fish" for containers, some of which contained money. The containers were either red or green, and for each subject only one color was rewarded. Subjects were divided into two conditions. In the Easy condition subjects used a horseshoe magnet to obtain containers located beneath a piece of cardboard, and using the magnets subjects had very little trouble in obtaining the containers, spending an average of only 14 seconds for each container. In the Hard condition subjects were required to lower a string though a hole in the cardboard and catch the containers with a hook on the end of the string. The latter task proved to be difficult, requiring an average of 52 seconds. Conceptually, what does this procedure mean?

Subjects in the Hard condition exerted considerable effort to no avail approximately half of the time. A container of one color, either green or red, was consistently not rewarded (contained no money). Dissonance should have been created between the individual's knowledge that he exerted considerable effort to obtain containers of color X and the knowledge that they contained no money. How will cognitive dissonance be reduced in Aronson's experimental design? Conceptually, subjects will reduce dissonance either by the addition of consonant elements or the subtraction of dissonant elements. In the present case we may define as consonant any cognitive elements consistent with the behavioral commitment of fishing. It would follow that the subject could then reduce dissonance by minimizing his estimate of the amount of effort and discomfort involved in the task, or else by enhancing the virtues of some aspect of the situation. Aronson focused on the latter and argued that the subject would show a tendency toward increased liking for the color of the unrewarded container. Relative to the Easy condition, this is precisely what subjects in the Hard condition did.

This experiment has demonstrated that a barrier (Hard condition) enhances the attractiveness of the difficult-to-obtain container, but only to the degree that the container is relatively *un*attractive (contains no money). The results are entirely in agreement with the dissonance analysis, which suggests that unjustified effort will create dissonance reduction. But it should be evident that the reactance derivation (and Wright's derivation) are directly contradicted. In this one important respect, reactance and dissonance theories are in contradiction, and the following discussion will attempt to clarify the reasons for this.

TOWARD UNDERSTANDING THE CONFLICT

It will be argued that the conflict can be resolved by appealing to the notion of decision, or behavioral commitment. Dissonance theory applies strictly to postdecisional phenomena, while reactance theory (plus Feather and Wright) generally deals with the person who has not yet decided. Regarding reactance theory, an important point should be made. The reactance phenomena studied thus far have been predecisional in the sense of the barrier or social influence coming prior to an overt decision. However, the *measure* of reactance does not necessarily need to be predecisional, even though it usually is, since reactance effects may easily carry over beyond the decision point. This was the essence of the argument employed when the dissonance paradigm was given a reactance interpretation. In order to further the contrast between the two theories, an example will be helpful.

Assume that a man is in either of the following situations. He takes his wife to see a movie, knowing full well that it is a superb movie, and true to his expectations the movie is indeed the best he has ever seen. In the second situation he takes his wife to the movie knowing that it is a foreign film, certainly not something he would enjoy. Almost anyone who has read dissonance theory would say that there is more dissonance arousal in the second situation than in the first. It is assumed implicitly in such a dissonance analysis that the behavioral commitment of attending the movie is a cognition highly resistant to change, and that cognitions dissonant with the commitment, such as the knowledge that the movie is abominable, will raise dissonance. How will dissonance be reduced? In situations such as this dissonance researchers have argued that an increased appreciation for the goal will result: That is, the movie will increase in attractiveness to the degree that it was initially undesirable.

This analysis in no way presumes that dissonance reduction results only after the *behavior*, but it is crucial for the theory that the person *decides* to attend the movie. The theory has an ambiguous application unless there has been a behavioral commitment.

To complete the example one more element is necessary—the presence or absence of a barrier. In the present case imagine that the man must drive with his wife for 30 miles, or alternatively, the movie is being shown at his neighbor's house.

Now, what happens to the attractiveness of the movie when a barrier is introduced, and how is this effect mediated by the initial attractiveness of the movie? Figure 5 describes the relationship as would be predicted from dissonance theory and also as predicted from reactance theory. Obviously the predictions are opposite, and the question is whether or not they are reconcilable.

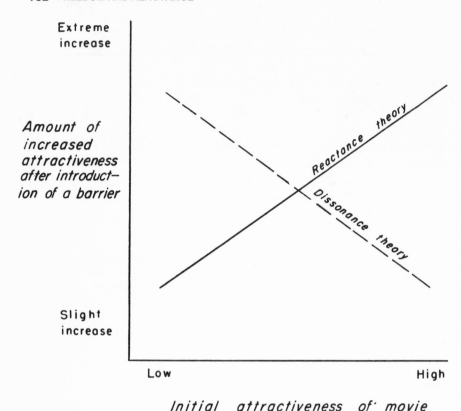

Fig. 5. Differentiating reactance and dissonance theories with the mediating variable "Initial Attractiveness."

One possibility is that the domain of the two types of theory is not overlapping. Dissonance theory applies only to the postdecisional period, and we should consider the consequences of assuming momentarily that reactance theory is only a theory of predecisional processes. This would imply a sequential effect. When the barrier is introduced before the person's decision we can predict the relationship specified by reactance theory. But then, at the point of behavioral commitment there is a reversal in the effect. Assuming the barrier does not cease to exist, the man will now justify his choice of a poor alternative more so than he would have justified his choice of a good one, in line with dissonance principles.

Returning to the example of the man who takes his wife to the movie, we might try to look at the situation from his perspective both before and after commitment. Prior to commitment he sees a clear choice: He can stay home, or he can go to the movie. Well before he makes up his mind the barrier is introduced—someone informs him of the 30-mile drive. It is not hard to imagine that he will be more upset in the case of an attractive movie, for the potential loss is greater in this case of an important freedom. In short, his efforts to reassert freedom will be more intense when the goal is attractive.

The psychological significance of the barrier is considerably different once the commitment has taken place. This we can see by playing the role of the movie-goer as well as by referring to dissonance theory. Imagine that the man has already committed himself to seeing the foreign film, the one he dislikes, with the knowledge that he must travel 30 miles to see it. Voluntarily he has placed himself into a most inconvenient situation, and the only obvious way to handle the dilemma is to tell himself that there are some redeeming virtures. In other words, he will come to appreciate the movie, and more so when the movie was hardly worth seeing at the outset.

In the terms of this example it may be easier to appreciate the pre–post-decision distinction. The psychological processes are entirely different. In the case of the predecisional, or reactance processes, the motivation is to regain something valued, and the more valued that quantity initially, the higher the motivation. Following the decision, the barrier has a different effect. The man is not trying to regain anything by his dissonance-reducing processes, but instead he is justifying his commitment to a nearly absurd and difficult activity.

Chapter 16 will delve into these sequential processes in more detail. As will then be suggested, the predecisional phase appears to be a time of emphasizing one's freedom and avoiding any possible losses. In fact, this motivation to avoid loss of freedoms seems to carry over slightly beyond the point of decision. Following commitment, the psychological processes turn to rationalization. The worse the chosen situation, the more the individual attempts to make it psychologically livable.

The preceding remarks are an effort to reconcile the two theories with respect to the variable of initial attractiveness of alternatives. In this one respect they obviously offer different predictions. At the same time, it might be remembered that the motive in this chapter has been one of unification. Virtually all of the forced-compliance phenomena make as much sense within a reactance theory context as within dissonance theory, and this is because none of those forced-compliance studies are necessarily post-decisional, except with respect to measurement. At this point attention will be turned briefly to Feather and Wright.

THE PRESENT STATUS OF TWO OTHER THEORIES

The potential applications of Feather's and Wright's notions were anticipated in Chapter 10. It was noted that Wright's notion about initial attractiveness overlaps somewhat with the importance-of-freedom dimension, and so does his idea of cognitive overlap. The research has supported

Wright's parallels to the importance variable, but of course there is nothing in his theory related to the dimension of freedom.

On the other hand, Feather's theory touches both on the freedom and importance variables, although the parallels are limited. Feather's specific form of the freedom variable, "ego-involvement," has been investigated directly, and so has his specific form of the importance variable, "achievement orientation."

Obviously both of these theories are directly relevant to the threat variable, and it was seen in Chapter 11 that they overlapped completely with reactance theory. But once other theoretical variables were drawn in (Chapters 12 and 13), it became apparent that reactance theory was more general. There are other sources of generality in the theory, and attention will now be given to one of those in a short chapter on proportion of freedom threatened.

14
PROPORTION OF FREEDOM
THREATENED BY BARRIERS

One of the central propositions of reactance theory has to do with the proportion of freedoms eliminated. As noted in Chapter 6, proportion can be defined in either of two ways: The number of free behaviors can be held constant while the number eliminated is varied, or vice versa. In an experiment by Brehm, McQuown, and Shaban (reported in Brehm, 1966) the number eliminated (one) was a constant while the total number of alternatives was either three or six. According to the theory, an elimination of one-third of an individual's freedoms should create more reactance than an elimination of one-sixth of his freedoms.

The subjects were eighth-grade students of both sexes, and the study was conducted in the school classrooms. In the first session all subjects completed a questionnaire asking them to rate six movies on the basis of short descriptions. The questionnaire simply asked the subjects how much they would like to see each movie. In the interim between the two sessions a booklet was prepared for each subject such that some subjects could be given a list of all six movies while other subjects could be presented with a list of their favorite three movies from the six rated initially. At the beginning of the second experimental session the subjects were reminded that the experimenter was interested in their evaluations of the movies, then the booklets were distributed. Choice-condition subjects were told that they would be able to select any one of the movies listed in the booklet and view it in a few days, while No-Choice-condition subjects were informed that a movie would be randomly selected for them. Then subjects were asked to fill out the questionnaire, and in the control condition, which was a Choice–Three Alternative condition with no movies eliminated, subjects proceeded with the questionnaire. In the "elimination" conditions an assistant entered the room before subjects began to complete the questionnaire, pretended to whisper something in the experimenter's ear, then the experimenter turned to the class and announced that one of the movies did not arrive with the others and would not be available for viewing. Because it was desired that the second-ranked alternative be restricted for all subjects, the experimenter went around the room and circled the unavailable (second-ranked) movie on each subject's booklet. The subjects were then instructed to complete the questionnaire.

Reactance should be aroused to the extent that a restriction is placed on viewing the second-ranked movie, and the reactance should be a positive function of the proportion of freedoms eliminated. This means that increased favorable ratings of the eliminated movie will be most frequent when one of *three* movies is eliminated. An analysis using mean rating changes did not show any reliable differences, but if the subjects are categorized according to whether they showed increased, decreased, or no change in rating, the following results emerge. Given that the alternative was eliminated, there was more increased favorable evaluation in the Three Alternative–Choice condition than in the Six Alternative–Choice condition, and further, the Three Alternative–Choice condition showed significantly more increase than did the Three Alternative–No Choice condition (see Table 30). The no-elimination control condition was almost significantly less than the Three Alternative–Choice condition, and thus, in summary, the results are entirely consistent with the predictions. It might also be noted that the proportion variable had no effect within the No Choice condition.

As in other experiments, the overall amount of decreased favorable evaluation was substantial: Even in the Three Alternative–Choice condition 31% of the subjects showed lowered ratings.

In summary, the proportion of freedoms threatened proves to be a determinant of reactance arousal, just as in the case of the social influence

TABLE 30

PERCENTAGE OF SUBJECTS WHO SHOWED INCREASED RATING

Condition	Percent
Choice	
Control (no elimination)	28
6 alternatives	11
3 alternatives	56
No Choice	
6 alternatives	9
3 alternatives	23

research. The present experiment makes the rather interesting point that reactance is maximal when the original number of alternatives is quite small, all other things being equal. This is an important conclusion, for it clarifies a possible misconception about reactance theory. The following example pursues this point.

Suppose a man interprets the U.S. Constitution as giving him an unalienable right to keep and bear arms. He then decides to go out and buy a gun. In one case he lives in an isolated village where his choice is between a .45 caliber pistol and a .38 caliber pistol. In a second case he lives in a major city, and although the .45 and .38 are his first and second-ranked choice alternatives, he is also free to choose among 28 other varieties of pistol. In short, the crucial difference between these two cases is in the number of alternatives. There is a sense in which one might say that more freedom exists in the second case. A "freedom = number of options" formula could be invoked. But reactance theory has never taken such a position.

If freedom were to be equated with number of options, what should happen if the man in the gun store discovers an exhorbitant tax attached to the .45? Defining amount of freedom in terms of number of alternatives, this threat will create the most reactance when he has 30 options from which to choose. But as the theory stands, the only prediction to be made from the 30 vs. 2 variable is in terms of proportion of freedom threatened. More reactance will result with a small number of alternatives, and the preceding experiment attests to this. Therefore, as yet, there is no basis for asserting that freedom is a function of number of alternatives.

15
A SPECIAL ISSUE: THE DIFFERENCE BETWEEN REACTANCE AND FRUSTRATION

AGGRESSION: A REFLECTION OF REACTANCE

The first 14 chapters depicted the freedom-robbed individual as the possessor of a goal-specific motivation—that of re-establishing the threatened freedom. The person was viewed as directly or indirectly attempting to re-create the possibility of a choice as free as the one existing prior to threats and usurpations. In the research on social influence and barriers, the behavior following threat to freedom was conceptualized as directed toward re-creating a previous free state of affairs, and in this sense such behaviors might be viewed as conservative. But in addition to the effort to regain freedom, other responses to reactance arousal can be construed. For a beginning, previous thinking in the area of frustration may lead to some hints.

Historically "frustration" has stood for a variety of events that disrupt goal-oriented activity. The definition of "goal-oriented activity" has been liberal and ranges from the runway endeavors of rats to protection of self-esteem. In many cases anecdotal and experimental operational definitions of frustration have coincided with restrictions to freedom, which means that it is sensible to inquire into the theoretical thinking about modes of reaction to frustration. Presumably these modes are simultaneously manifestations of reactance, provided of course that the frustrations in question are violations of freedom.

One of the more accepted proposals of psychology is called the "frustration-aggression hypothesis." In 1939 Dollard, Doob, Miller, Mowrer, and Sears published the often cited statement that aggression can be expected to the extent that a goal-oriented response is subject to interference (frustrated). The authors described three major determinants of the strength of aggressive responses produced by frustrations: (a) The stronger or more motivated the goal response, the more aggression; (b) more aggression results from more interference; and (c) frustration effects summate such that the aggressive response to a frustration will be greater when that response was previously frustrated. These three variables resemble some of the determinants of reactance, which means that we should not be surprised if aggression is an outcome of restricted freedom.

In the original statement of reactance theory Brehm indicated that certain phenomenological effects would accompany reactance, including awareness of hostile and aggressive feelings. From Brehm's statement we might infer that when restrictions are due to a social agent, one direct route to reassertion of freedom will be a direct attack on the restricting agent or upon his desires and values. Thus aggression and hostility could be implicated in the process of attempting to restore freedom.

The preceding reasoning would suggest that "instrumental" aggression will generally be a component of reactance effects when a social agent is the root of reactance. If someone demands that we contribute to a fund, an aggressive response is entailed by refusal; when a member of an audience attempts to ridicule a speaker, the speaker's freedom to present himself as he wishes is threatened, and the freedom-restoring castigation of the provocative audience member constitutes aggression.

If aggression is nothing but the direct reassertion of freedom in the context of a social incident, then aggression has no unique role in this discussion. Aggression would simply be the process of regaining freedom, and in that respect it is not conceptaully different from any other process of freedom-restoration. However, there is a second possibility: Buss (1961) draws a distinction between angry and instrumental aggression. Instrumental aggression involves harming, disliking, or otherwise acting against others incidentally; the goal of the activity is other than hurting someone. In terms of preceding examples the speaker who chastises his audience does not necessarily intend to injure anyone's pride, for his intent is to clear the way for an uninterrupted (free) presentation. The college professor may not give exams with the primary motive of injuring others, but a certain psychological trauma among students could be the inevitable outcome of the teacher's efforts to test his effectiveness in instilling knowledge. Thus the interesting possibility with respect to reactance processes is *angry* aggression. Is it possible that reactance can arouse aggression or hostility such that the goal is to injure another? Will reactance cause ill feelings and unkind behavior toward the source of restriction, even when such effects are not the direct product of efforts to restore freedom?

The distinction between angry and instrumental aggression should be reconsidered. How are the two to be distinguished? First, observation might render a categorization of behavior into instrumental vs. angry aggression. If the aggression is at a more intensive level than would be required to restore freedom, or if aspects of the behavior make it obvious that the purpose is personal injury, we might have some confidence in labeling the behavior as angry. Second, if we consider *hostility* (i.e., the attitude corresponding to aggression rather than aggression itself), it seems unlikely that hostility could ever be instrumental in regaining freedom. *Aggressive behavior* can directly serve the end of renewed freedom, but a *hostile attitude* toward a social agent of restriction would seem to accomplish nothing in the way of reasserting freedom. To the extent that hostility is a direct outcome of reactance arousal it is a unique subject of study, for it does not fall into the conceptual class of behaviors and attitudes aimed toward re-establishing freedom.

THE ROLE OF EXPECTATION

A number of authors (Bateson, 1941; Berkowitz, 1962; Cohen, 1955; Kregarman & Worchel, 1961; Pastore, 1950, 1952; Zander, 1944) have qualified the frustration-aggression hypothesis with the notion that aggression results only to the degree that the frustration comes as a surprise, is inappropriate, or more generally, is unexpected. The language varies, but the central idea is that unanticipated frustration is more likely to produce aggression. The evidence for this proposition is fairly convincing and comes from diverse forms of research.

This notion of expectation should be compared with the concept of freedom. An example based on an experiment by Kregarman and Worchel (1961) will be helpful. The authors created a classroom situation where subjects would be tested and could potentially be berated and distracted by the tester. At the outset of the testing session a differential expectation was created so that subjects either expected the tester to distract and insult them or else had no such expectation. The experimenter then proceeded to distract the subjects. The results showed that hostility toward the experimenter as measured by a paper-and-pencil test was generated to the extent that the frustration was unexpected.

In this experiment the subjects did not necessarily have freedom to be interrupted or not to be interrupted. That was not a choice for them to make. But a choice could have been built into the situation, such that subjects could have chosen at any point to have someone distract and interrupt them, or not. Had the experiment been designed in this way the interruption would have threatened a freedom and generated reactance. If Brehm (1966) is right, this reactance should elicit hostility toward the interrupter. Moreover, this react-ance-produced hostility should *add to* the hostility resulting from the violation of expectancy.

Summary To sum up: It has been argued previously that frustration alone is insufficient to produce aggression. When that frustration is unexpected, aggression is more likely. Finally, when that unexpected frustration also constitutes a threat to freedom, the resulting reactance will add to the aggression. The following experiment by Worchel (1971) translates this reasoning into an empirical test.

An Experiment on Frustration, Expectancy, and Choice[1]

Design. The major purpose of the study was that of separating the effects of simple frustration, violation of expectancy, and loss of freedom. As with earlier research the present experiment defined freedom in terms of choice, which means that some subjects (*Choice* condition) were told they could select any of three alternatives. Subjects in the remaining two conditions were given no choice and were distinguished in the following way: In the *Expectancy* condition subjects were led to expect to receive whichever alternative was most attractive; in the *No Expectancy* condition, subjects had no idea which alternative they would receive.

The second variable was the attractiveness of the alternative received. Based on a premeasure of item attractiveness each subject was assigned an alternative by the experimenter, this alternative being either the first, second, or third-rated item.

The dependent measure consisted of hostility directed toward the experimenter who assigned the subject an alternative. By looking at the design with this measure in mind, we can consider the psychological impact of the various experimental combinations. (1) *Choice* condition: No matter which alternative the subject receives, his freedom of choice is violated by virtue of the assignment being made without his consent. Thus if hostility results from reactance, there should be hostility to the degree that the subject receives an unattractive alternative. The reasoning here is simply that the freedom to possess an object is important when the object is attractive (cf. Chapter 13). Therefore, an important freedom is usurped when an unattractive alternative is received. (2) *Expectancy* condition: Since the subject expects to receive the first-rated alternative his expectancy should be disconfirmed only when he receives the second or third-rated object. There should be no hostility when the first-rated object is awarded to him, for in that case there is no deviation from expectancy. Therefore, there should definitely be a difference between the Choice and the Expectancy conditions when the highest-rated item is received, and the difference should be due to reactance. Hostility should also be greater in the Choice than in the Expectancy condition when the second or

---

[1]Since the Worchel study has not yet been published its method and results will be given a detailed treatment.

TABLE 31

SUMMARY OF PSYCHOLOGICAL PROCESSES LEADING TO HOSTILITY
IN THE CONDITIONS OF WORCHEL'S EXPERIMENT

Condition	Attractiveness of alternative received		
	Most attractive	Second most attractive	Least attractive
Choice	1. no frustration	1. frustration	1. frustration
	2. no disconfirmed expectancy	2. disconfirmation of expectancy	2. disconfirmation of expectancy
	3. restricted freedom	3. restricted freedom	3. restricted freedom
Expectancy	1. no frustration	1. frustration	1. frustration
	2. no disconfirmed expectancy	2. disconfirmed expectancy	2. disconfirmed expectancy
No expectancy	1. no frustration	1. frustration	1. frustration

third-rated alternative is received. This is because the Choice subjects should have expected to receive the best through free choice, thus an expectancy is denied for them just as it is for the Expectancy subjects, but in addition, the effects of reactance add to the effects of deviation from expectancy. (3) *No Expectancy* condition: If hostility is the result of a simple frustration, hostility should result only when the second or third-rated item is received. This hypothesis assumes that the first-ranked item is the person's desired goal and that the deletion of that goal is a frustration. Since these subjects have no specific expectation, their hostility will be a function of pure frustration without the added effects of deviation from expectation and reactance. Therefore, there should be less hostility in this condition than in the Expectancy or Choice conditions, no matter which item is received.

These predictions can best be understood by reference to Table 31, which separates the processes taking place within each condition. Note that reactance is the only process within the condition where the most attractive alternative is received, and that in the conditions where the second most attractive and least attractive alternatives are received the three processes (frustration, deviation from expectancy, and reactance) add to one another as the focus is shifted from the No Expectancy condition to the Expectancy and then to the Choice condition.

Procedure. The subjects were undergraduate males from introductory psychology classes. At the time subjects signed up they were given to believe that they would receive either a gift or cash for their participation in an experiment on "motivation and performance."

Subjects were run individually. The experimenter described the study as an investigation of the effects of different varieties of incentives on task performance. He noted that the subject would be asked to perform two tasks during the experimental session and would be compensated by one of three available incentives: one hour experimental credit, five dollars, or a bottle of men's cologne. At this point the *premeasure* was handed to the subject for the purpose of establishing a measure of attractiveness of the three incentives, then the manipulation of choice and expectancy was performed.

(1) *Choice* condition: The subject was led to expect a free choice among the three alternatives later in the session. (2) *Expectancy* condition: In every case the subject was promised the alternative that he had rated highest. The instructions were given so that the subject would not think his premeasure ratings determined that he would receive the highest. (3) *No Expectancy* condition: Subjects were told that an assistant who they would meet later in the session was responsible for deciding which alternative would be given.

The experimenter then set the stage for the dependent measure. The subject was told that he would go upstairs and meet an assistant who would instruct him in the performance of the tasks and give him the incentive. The experimenter said that subjects were being asked to rate the assistant on several dimensions since a number of individuals were being considered for the job of assistant. Thus the subject expected to go upstairs, meet the assistant, perform the task, receive the incentive, and then finally go to a designated room to rate the assistant.

Consistent with instructions the subject went to the assistant who showed him how to carry out the two tasks. Once they had been completed he told all the subjects the following:

This completes the experiment. You will get the _____ (either the first, second, or third-ranked alternative). I've decided to try and give out equal numbers of each incentive, so you'll get this one.

The preceding remarks constituted the manipulation of item given, in that the subject received either the first, second, or third-ranked alternative.

After the subject had been awarded the appropriate incentive he went to a predesignated room and filled out some rating forms. Central to this discussion is the "assistant evaluation questionnaire," which asked the subject to evaluate the assistant on the following dimensions: efficiency, smoothness of experimental conduct, pleasantness, likableness, and whether or not the assistant should be considered for the job. Although Worchel analyzed the data from all five questions, he placed primary emphasis on the

TABLE 32
MEAN HOSTILITY SCORES[a]
(SHOULD ASSISTANT BE CONSIDERED FOR THE JOB)

Condition	Attractiveness of alternative received		
	Most attractive	Second most attractive	Least attractive
Choice	13.57	17.07	22.21
Expectancy	10.50	10.00	14.36
No expectancy	11.40	9.50	10.50

[a] A high number indicates high hostility. In terms of the specific question, a high number means that the subject does not want the assistant to be hired.

"should be considered for the job" item, since it stated directly whether or not the assistant should be hired and asked the subject to take everything about the assistant into account. It was worded as follows:

> Everything considered, do you think this person would make a good experimenter and should be seriously considered for the job of research assistant?

To answer this question the subject placed a check mark on a scale with end points labeled "very definitely yes" and "very definitely no."[2]

Results. In Table 32 the mean hostility ratings are presented for the nine conditions such that a high number indicates high hostility. First we will examine hostility as a function of which alternative was received. Within the No Expectancy condition there was no effect for alternative received. This means there is no support in this context for the contention that a simple frustration (devoid of expectancy and choice) generates hostility. Within the Expectancy condition there is some evidence that a strong violation of expectancy makes a difference in that more hostility was evident in the Least Attractive condition than in the Second Most Attractive condition ($p < .01$). In

[2] This dependent measure is called a "hostility" measure because it presumably reflects the subject's attitude toward the target. The distinction drawn between aggression and hostility has to do with overt behavior. "Aggression" in this chapter is considered to be overt behavior directed toward someone, whereas "hostility" is the attitude basic to such aggression.

the Choice condition the attractiveness of the alternative received made a great deal of difference. Table 32 indicates that hostility increased as attractiveness of the received alternative decreased. The difference between the Most Attractive and Second Most Attractive conditions was significant ($p < .05$), and so was the difference between the Second Most Attractive and Least Attractive conditions ($p < .01$).

Second, we should examine the differences as a function of the choice-expectancy variable. Comparing the No Expectancy and Expectancy conditions, there is a significant difference only when the least attractive alternative is received ($p < .05$). Apparently a violation of expectancy, even when not involving freedom of choice, will generate hostility when the deviation from expectancy is sufficiently strong. Comparing the Expectancy and Choice conditions it is evident that violation of a free choice has a stronger impact than mere disruption of an expectancy. There is a reliable difference between the Expectancy and Choice conditions for both the second most attractive ($p < .001$) and least attractive alternatives ($p < .001$), and a similar but not quite significant effect ($.05 < p < .10$) was found for the most attractive alternative.

CHAPTER SUMMARY

There has never been any convincing evidence that a simple frustration, devoid of strong expectancy and of freedom of choice, can produce a hostile reaction. Early research was so complex that the frustrations were violations of expectancies and of free choices as well as simple frustrations. In the research specifically concerned with expectancy (e.g., Kregarman & Worchel, 1961) this problem was handled partially, although freedom of choice was not clearly disentangled from expectancy in those projects. Thus even in the considerable research involving a manipulation of expectancy there was no good evidence that hostility is differentially affected by violations of expectancy and violations of free choice.

The Worchel experiment was designed specifically to separate the three processes of simple frustration (thwarting), deviation from expectancy, and reactance, and was accomplished in such a way that the simple frustration involved neither a deviation from a definite expectancy nor a restriction of freedom. The results indicated rather clearly that the contribution of restricted freedom to hostility is considerable. There was no apparent relationship between pure frustration and hostility, and the contribution of violated expectancy was minimal. The restriction of a free choice had a much greater impact than violation of expectancy and was evident no matter which alternative was forced upon the subject.

Earlier, the distinction between instrumental and angry aggression was discussed with reference to reactance theory. In that discussion it became apparent that instrumental aggression was a necessary component of reactance in many cases, and the major question was whether or not angry aggression and hostility would be an outcome of reactance. Since there is no necessary theoretical connection between hostility and reassertion of freedom the question needed to be decided by a research effort, and Worchel's experiment seems conclusive. However, there may be some possibility of interpreting the hostility results in terms of instrumental actions, by using the concept of generalization.

To react to a threat to freedom with aggressive behavior can often be useful. If such aggression eliminates the source of threat or otherwise reduces threat, restoration of freedom is directly served. But this form of instrumental aggression can be effective only when the threat can be dealt with. If a child's freedom to play with his own toys is threatened by a second child, reactance may well be manifested in aggression directed toward the threatener. If such aggression reduces the threat, the instrumental value is obvious. But this is a much different case from the Worchel paradigm, where the hostility that was expressed was objectively pointless from an instrumental standpoint. The freedom had been eliminated for good, and certainly the subject's questionnaire responses would have been ineffective in reestablishing freedom. However, Worchel's subjects could have been generalizing. From earlier experiences with the successful confrontation of threats, subjects may have generalized to the case of *eliminated* freedom and shown hostility even though to do so was not directly effective.

This interpretation has a more extended implication. With respect to reactance the angry aggression vs. instrumental aggression distinction may not be at all useful, for it falters for at least three reasons: (*a*) The dividing line between "potentially instrumental" and "potentially not instrumental" is a thin one. The observer surely would find it difficult to assess accurately the aggressive person's potential for meeting the threat effectively. (*b*) If the instrumental vs. angry distinction is made from the subject's standpoint there is again an arbitrariness. Some people who flail out with aggressive actions may believe that their actions are instrumental in the regaining of freedom, and some may not. And certainly there is no reason to expect people to understand when their freedom-restoration efforts will be effective. (*c*) The most important point is this: All aggression that results in response to freedom-limitation may have its psychological origin in the motivation to reassert freedom. Whether or not aggression (or hostility) *in fact* becomes instrumental to threat removal or threat reduction is perhaps of negligible import as far as the psychological state of the threatened person is concerned. A threat or usurpation of freedom might generally set off an aggressive or hostile reaction toward the threatener, motivated by the desire to regain the freedom.

Moving away from the angry-instrumental issue, Worchel's experiment provides a strong basis for re-interpreting previous findings of frustration-aggression. It seems possible that many instances of frustration are simultaneously restrictions of freedom. The aggressive reactions stemming from those cases could easily be either actual efforts to reassert freedom, or responses deriving from and related to reassertion attempts. Apparently, the passive, unfree person, devoid of personal control over his situation has little or no potential for hostile and aggressive behavior.

wrong

— it is often the most helpless (subjectively experienced) who have the greatest capacity for intropunitive or extrapunitive hostility + aggression

16
SELF-IMPOSED THREATS TO FREEDOM

In previous chapters there is evidence that external factors such as social influence attempts and barriers can threaten freedom, but it may also be true that threats can originate from within. Wicklund (1968, 1970) has noted that a person's felt preferences can carry threats to his own freedoms. Linder and Crane (1970) and Linder et al. (1971) have elaborated on this notion in the context of some experimental research, and the reasoning behind the idea of self-imposed threats was spelled out in Chapter 1.

When a person has freedom to select a course of action he is necessarily in a position to eliminate his own freedom. Once he embarks on an irreversible commitment he is no longer free to select those alternatives he has rejected, and this loss should produce reactance, just as barriers bring forth reactance. These post-commitment manifestations of reactance are labeled "regret," and will be studied shortly. The analysis of self-imposed freedom elimination seems straightforward, but what about threats that do not constitute eliminations?

If irreversible decisions eliminate freedoms, self-imposed threats to freedom that *do not eliminate* freedom must necessarily occur prior to the commitment point. It is suggested here that threats to freedom arise when the person adopts preferences among alternatives, for such preferences imply future loss (elimination) of freedom. When the woman in Chapter 1 came to prefer one suitor over another, the preference was said to imply the eventual loss of her other suitor. Therefore, the stronger her preference, the greater the threat to that alternative freedom.

The point about the effect of a preference might be made more general. If the person has done something implying that a decision alternative will be eliminated, reactance will be aroused. The stronger that implication, the more reactance. Numerous kinds of influences may affect the strength of that implication, such as the irrevocability of his statement of preference or his proximity to the decision. Decision proximity is studied in some detail in experiments to follow, and the reasoning behind it was explicated in Chapter 1.

The point is simply that a preference carries a stronger implication for action (and loss of freedom) when the commitment is near at hand.

All of the reactance-theory variables studied previously apply to the case of self-imposed threats, although the research conducted under this rubric has not been extensive and just a few of those variables are introduced. Freedom, the many-faceted importance of freedom, proportion of freedom threatened, and implications for future threats all apply here exactly as before.

How is a self-imposed threat to freedom reasserted? Nothing new is required for this analysis, for reassertion simply means directly engaging in threatened behaviors and becoming more attracted to those behaviors. When a preference for Alternative A comes into existence and thereby threatens the freedom to select Alternative B, B should subsequently become more attractive while A would fall in attractiveness.

There is one logical trick regarding the measurement. If Alternative B is increased to a point where A is superseded, then A becomes threatened. That reactance would then cause Alternative A to be raised, and if increased above B, B would again be threatened, etc., *ad infinitum*. If this oscillation process actually occurs, the measurement problems would be imposing. However, it is unlikely that such oscillation would continue for long. There is reason to think that the amplitude of the oscillations would fall off rapidly, because an eventual equating of the attractiveness of the alternatives would, more than any other result, benefit the person who desires to preserve his freedom. Only the complete absence of a preference would minimize the self-imposed threat to freedom. This "convergence" has been the focus of research by Linder and Crane (1970), and Linder et al. (1971), and was first suggested by them.

Before proceeding, some discussion will be given to the concept of "decision," which is vital in this analysis of self-imposed threats.

THE DECISION

"Loss of freedom" is the ultimate, limiting case of threat. It has just been argued that freedom is lost, usurped, or eliminated once the individual has irreversibly committed himself to an alternative. This ultimate loss is, of course, not necessary for reactance arousal. A preference can threaten the person with eventual or possible loss, and this is why preferences might create reactance. Preferences are generally viewed as being predecisional, whereas the loss of freedom is a postdecisional fact. However, to apply the theory there is no necessity of understanding precisely at what point the commitment takes place, nor is there any reason to delve into the ultimate meaning of the concept "decision." The reasoning for this statement is as follows.

"Threat to freedom" is a continuous variable. The weakest possible threat exists if the person feels some slight potential infringement upon his freedom, whereas the ultimate threat occurs upon an actual usurpation of freedom. Within the decision-making context this continuous property can be explicated easily. For example, if a person states his preference in an indecisive, questioning, or tentative manner, there is not a very strong implication for eventual loss of specific options. If he states his preference in a more definite way, the implication is stronger. If he signs a contract eliminating all options except one, the implication is as strong as possible. Now, the question arises, at what point has a person decided? Must his statement be public? Must he take some motor action toward the alternatives, indicating his definite acceptance of one? Can a strong statement of preference sometimes be a decision? For reactance theory none of these questions are of much consequence. The only question of crucial importance is this: When a person shows a preference for an alternative, moves toward it, or in any way demonstrates his biases for it, how strong an implication exists *for him* that other alternatives are endangered as options?

A contrast between reactance and dissonance theories will be helpful on this point. As should have been apparent from the earlier discussion of cognitive-dissonance theory, dissonance phenomena are primarily post-decisional. To use dissonance theory unambiguously it is important to establish that a person has already decided. The clearest definition of "decision" within the dissonance context seems to be that of Festinger in 1964, where he acknowledged that dissonance can be aroused by a statement of preference, provided that the person is aware of the alternatives at the time of preference. But there is a trick: Festinger also noted that dissonance *reduction* would not ensue due to a simple preference. First the deciding person must know which alternatives he will receive and which he will forego. In other words, some action more definitive than a statement of preference is necessary.

Reactance is aroused by a statement of preference, or by a more definitive statement of preference, or by a totally irreversible commitment, ánd the amount of reactance increases from the former to the latter. The important contrast with dissonance is that reactance will be manifested in direct proportion to the strength of implication for eventual loss, while dissonance processes do not bear a monotonic relation to the "decisiveness" or "unequivocality" of the preference. Only when the outcomes of the decision are known for sure will dissonance reduction begin.

With these introductory remarks, attention will now be given to some theoretical ideas that parallel or contradict the self-imposed threat notion. These ideas will be carried into the discussion of the research in order to show precisely in which ways they differ with the reactance concept.

THEORIES APPLICABLE TO THE DECISION-MAKING PROCESSES

Conflict—N. E. Miller

Typically, the notion of decision *per se* has been excluded from discussions of conflict as associated with Miller's (1944) treatment, but for all practical purposes "goal attainment" can be equated with "decision" in the present context. The central ideas of the theory have to do with the concept of "goal gradient." "Goal gradient" means that the approach and avoidance components in the organism's behavior will become more intense as the organism comes nearer to the goal. In terms of running speed or persistence this would mean that a goal with only an approach component (containing nothing to motivate avoidance behavior) will be approached more rapidly or diligently as the organism draws near to it. Conversely, a goal with only negative characteristics will increase in its aversive power as the organism comes near. In order to loosen up Miller's analysis for the present application, increased speed of approach or diligence might be translated into "goal attractiveness." Such a translation is questionable, but it will be proposed for the time being. Using the notion of "goal attractiveness" to replace "approach," and "goal unattractiveness" to replace "avoidance," we will provide an example to show how the theory applies to decision-making and to elucidate some details of Miller's theory.

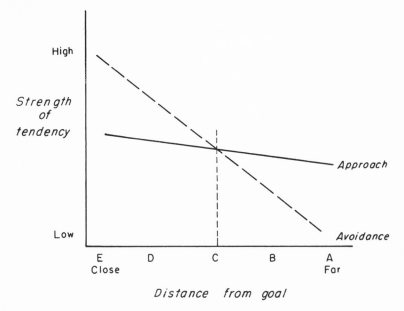

Fig. 6. Strength of approach and avoidance tendencies and distance from goal.

Assume a person in a cafeteria line is confronted with two desserts of approximately equal attractiveness and equally distant from him. No theory could very well predict which one he will initially move toward, but assuming that each dessert carries just an approach component, the behavior is predictable once he begins to reach for one. The goal-gradient idea says that the strength of approach behavior is inversely proportional to the distance between the person and the goal; thus, an initial preference will be followed by an increasingly strong differential preference.

Once there is an element to avoid in the decision-making situation the theorizing becomes more complex. In addition to assuming that strength of avoidance is inversely proportional to distance from the goal, Miller also assumes that the distance-avoidance relationship is of a different nature from the distance-approach relationship. As illustrated in Fig. 6, he proposes that the avoidance component rises more sharply than does the approach component. Literally translated, Fig. 6 simply states that tendencies to avoid the goal increase quickly as the goal is approached, but tendencies to approach increase slowly.[1]

Figure 6 captures the essence of the predecisional convergence phenomenon illustrated in the example in Chapter 1 of the woman having to choose between two suitors. As the person approaches the goal, there is an increasing tendency for attraction to lower rated alternatives to increase, relative to the initially most desired alternative.[2] It is important to keep in mind that Miller's analysis assumes a definite aversive element in the situation—something that would set up an avoidance gradient with respect to the most preferred alternative as the subject comes close. Looking back to the preceding example, such an avoidance gradient might be created by an offensive odor set off by the dessert.

There is a problem here. Many of the experimental situations to which reactance theory has been applied contain no obvious avoidance gradients. In fact one study even deals with exotic desserts (Brehm & Rozen, 1971). Throughout the research to be reviewed avoidance gradients would have to be imputed, for aversive elements are anything but conspicuous. But as it turns

---

[1]The assumption has an interesting rationale. When an organism approaches a goal it does so because of (a) external factors, especially the sight, sound, and smell of the goal, and also because of (b) internal factors, such as hunger, thirst, sex drive, or whatever led it to the choice situation in the first place. Since a substantial portion of its motion toward the goal is attributable to these internal factors, it is reasonable that distance from the goal does not radically affect the approach tendency, since such factors are constant. The fact that there is any approach gradient at all is explained by Miller as a result of external stimuli; for example, the organism might break into a run as the delicious smell of a dessert becomes noticeable.

[2]Literally translated, the figure says that attraction to the initially preferred goal declines as the person approaches it. But this may be taken to mean that other alternatives increase in attractiveness relative to that preferred initially.

out, Miller supplies a way to impute an avoidance gradient into *any* choice situation.

Miller indicates that an approach-approach conflict can be translated into a double approach-avoidance conflict by assuming that the potential loss of a decision alternative is aversive. Unlike the aversive component of the objectionable smell of a dessert, a quality inherent in the choice alternative, the anticipation of loss is a component carried around with the person and should become salient whenever something valuable is to be lost. Looking at the Chapter 1 example from this perspective, the predecisional convergence begins to make sense in the Miller framework. Even though the two alternative men may have been totally lacking in objectionable qualities, the ultimate approach of one could have been aversive due to anticipated renunciation of the other.

The Miller Extension: A Summing Up

The present extension of Miller's model seems to apply readily to self-imposed threat effects. But there are two serious reservations concerning this application: (a) The equation of "approach" with "attractiveness" and the equation of "avoidance" with "unattractiveness" are highly debatable. Within Miller's framework "attractiveness" of alternatives is an integral component of them, and as such is not said to vary as the organism approaches the goal. Running speed may increase as the goal is approached, but Miller would not thereby conclude that attractiveness also increases. (b) An important assumption granted by Miller (1944) is that an avoidance gradient can be set up by the organism's anticipated loss of an attractive goal object. This assumption was relied upon heavily for the present extension of Miller, since much of the subsequent research contains no obvious avoidance elements, such as bad smell or electric shocks. However, it is probably an error to place so much emphasis on Miller's 1944 assumption. That assumption creates a serious difficulty for his theory, for the clarity of the approach and avoidance elements is muddled if the assumption is carried into all applications. And it does look as though Miller was only temporarily driven to this assumption, for it does not reappear in his later statement of the theory (Miller, 1959).

In short, Miller's theory as applied to the present research is equivocal. In a gross sense the theory can easily be made to predict a predecisional convergence, but there are weaknesses that result from making the theory cognitive. Keeping in mind these weaknesses, we will invoke the conflict extension at various points in the subsequent discussion of research, in order to contrast it with the reactance interpretation.

Choice Certainty—Mills

The notion of choice certainty implies an effect exactly opposite from that of reactance theory, and for this reason Mills' ideas will be carried into this chapter in order to try to assess which is correct under what kind of circumstances. On the assumption that people desire to be certain that their chosen courses of action are correct, Mills (1965, 1968) has formulated a theory of choice certainty that extends both to selective exposure to information and evaluative changes in choice alternatives. In the present section just his comments on evaluative changes will be treated; selective exposure will be discussed later in the chapter.

As extended in a paper by O'Neal and Mills (1969), the theory of choice certainty assumes that people want to be certain, upon deciding, that they are selecting the best possible course of action. The less their certainty, the more attempts will be made to increase it. If a person is confronted with a decision, and some of his cognitions imply taking one action while other cognitions imply the opposite, he can be expected to change his cognitions in such a way that the favored alternative becomes increasingly favored. Stated differently, the choice alternatives will be spread apart in attractiveness, and this phenomenon reflects the desire to be certain of making the correct choice as one approaches the decision point.

Adding to the central postulate, Mills[3] stipulates that the predecisional divergence of alternatives will be more prevalent the closer the person is to committing himself. This is because the need to become certain becomes maximal as the necessity of engaging in commitment approaches.

The contrast between the reactance and choice-certainty approaches should be evident. One stipulates a tendency toward convergence of alternatives, especially as the commitment point approaches, while the other suggests exactly the opposite.

Predecisional Bolstering—Janis and Mann

Mann, Janis, and Chaplin (1969) have performed an experiment to test some ideas set forth by Janis and Mann (1968), and in the process they have proposed a model of predecisional conflict reduction. In many respects the model is similar to that of Mills. The authors view the person who is about to decide as in a state of tension, and they describe two routes by which the tension is lowered. First, new information can enter the picture, which will affect the ratings of the alternatives just as it affected them within the Miller and Mills theories. Second, given that no new information is expected, the individual can be expected to distort the attractiveness of the alternatives. Thus whether or not new information is forthcoming is a crucial variable within the Janis and Mann conception of the decision maker. The second variable is the

[3]Personal communication from Judson Mills.

person's confidence, and as we might expect, confidence acts just as certainty within Mills' analysis. Because the Janis and Mann model does not add anything to Mills' ideas within the context of this writing, only Mills will be referenced from here on.

As with the two previous models, there is never any reason to expect a reversal in preference once the individual has adopted an initial preference, unless, of course, new information directly leads to a reversal. The ideas of Mills and of Janis and Mann are in sharp contrast to the foregoing proposals. This is especially true in the case of Mills, who indicates that divergence of alternatives should increase as the choice point comes closer. Since reactance theory implies exactly the opposite, the research soon to be discussed will be especially informative regarding the particular cognitive processes surrounding the decision point.

Dissonance—Festinger

In 1964 Festinger introduced a modification of his original theory. He suggested that dissonance will often be manifested in "regret," defined operationally as a choice inversion or tendency toward choice inversion as indicated in ratings of the alternatives. The regret phase of decision making, which ensues once dissonance has been aroused, will directly reflect the magnitude of dissonance and eventually be superseded by dissonance reduction.

A person does not need to commit himself in the usual sense for there to be dissonance arousal. As will be discussed later, Festinger and Walster found that regret resulted from a mere pre-commitment ranking. The implication appears to be that any discrimination made among the alternatives can arouse dissonance in the decision maker and thereby bring forth regret. Furthermore, the greater the behavioral implications implicit in that statement of preference, the more dissonance will be aroused, and the more regret should be manifested. One crucial point must be kept in mind here: Dissonance *reduction* does not necessarily follow a dissonance arousal-regret sequence. Festinger (1964) allows that dissonance can be created through an implicit choice or statement of preference, with resultant regret, but dissonance *reduction* will be observed only if that statement of preference has clear implications for a course of action. In other terms, dissonance reduction is found only if the individual has definitely made up his mind among the alternatives and knows which ones will be received and which foregone.

In order to illustrate the operation of dissonance theory during the decision process we might examine Fig. 7. Assume that the person makes three distinct statements of preference during the course of the decision, the last one being the actual commitment. For the purpose of the example it is helpful to assume that dissonance dissipates after a short time, although such an

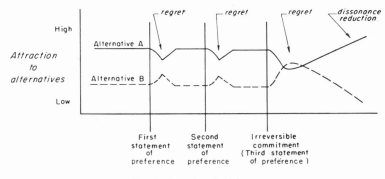

Fig. 7. Predecisional processes implied by Festinger's 1964 dissonance theory.

assumption is by no means necessary. The diagram illustrates the points that have been made above. A preference is followed by regret, which is manifested in a tendency for the alternatives to converge. Dissonance reduction follows only after a definite commitment.

Figure 7 illustrates the operation of dissonance theory independent of the introduction of new information about choice alternatives. Any new information would have to be categorized according to whether it was favorable or unfavorable to either alternative. It would then be a simple matter to predict whether dissonance would be greater or less, given a statement of preference.

The difficult part of the analysis is in the specification of when the regret-dissonance-reduction processes will begin. Just how strong must the statement of preference be in order for regret to ensue, and must the statement of preference be public? We can hardly specify the onset of regret at this stage of theorizing, except in extreme cases such as behavioral commitment or other strong statements of preference. Unless one of these extreme cases has occurred, the best we can do is to argue that the magnitude of regret and dissonance reduction, when they occur, will be directly related to the variables that maximize dissonance arousal.

Comparing the Dissonance and Reactance
Approaches to Convergence of Alternatives

The easiest place to find a parallel between the theories is at the period immediately following a definite decision. For different theoretical reasons, both ideas imply a postdecision "regret," defined as a convergence or tendency toward crossing-over of alternatives. In simple terms, the person appears to desire what he has just discarded. There is also a parallel between the two theories when simple statements of preference are made, independent of whether or not those statements constitute absolute commitments. Dissonance theory allows that the statement will produce dissonance and regret (convergence), while reactance theory indicates that the preference statement will threaten freedom and thereby result in convergence.

There is an important distinction to be drawn between the two approaches. As shown above, reactance theory directly implies that the self-imposed threat to freedom will be a function of decision proximity, but such a proximity variable is not contained within the dissonance-theory analysis of regret. There are other ways to distinguish the theories in terms of the variables specific to the two notions. One such discrimination is drawn in an experiment by Brehm and Wicklund (1970) to be discussed below.

EXPERIMENTAL RESEARCH

Reactance theory will be the basis for subdividing this section, and the research will be discussed under the topics "Strength of Threat," "Freedom," and "Importance of Freedom." Toward the end of each section some comments will be offered on the applicability of the other theoretical notions just considered. Following this research section there will be an elaboration on theoretical points touched on by the research.

Strength of Threat

How can the strength of threat to one's own freedom vary? In general, by the strength of the person's feeling that his current preferences imply a loss of freedom. Of the many ways to alter this feeling of implication for loss, one in particular is the focus here: proximity to decision.

Linder and Crane (1970) led their subjects to expect a decision and varied how much time subjects anticipated there would be prior to deciding. If the theoretical idea is correct, subjects who think they are near the decision point should fail to differentiate among the alternatives, in terms of attractiveness. To see the options as equally attractive is to give oneself the greatest possible freedom.

Female undergraduates were led to believe that they would be interviewed by a graduate student and that they would have a choice among the two interviewers. The subject first expected to read short descriptions of the two graduate students, and then to have a "get-acquainted" period with each one in order to better evaluate them before the choice.

The main experimental manipulation was the expected length of the get-acquainted period. At the time the subject was given brief descriptions of the two graduate students, she was told either that the period would be 3, 8, or 15 minutes long. Keeping in mind that the subject expected she would have to decide shortly after the get-acquainted period, it is obvious that the temporal independent variable is a manipulation of the distance, in time, from the point of commitment. As soon as the subject finished reading the two descriptions and had been given one of the three temporal instructions, she was asked to fill out a questionnaire indicating her preference among the two graduate students in terms of how much she would like to have an interview with each of them. In addition to the experimental variations there were two control conditions, but they need not be discussed here.

On the basis of reactance theory, the three experimental conditions should have shown progressively more convergence the closer in time the subject was to the decision; thus, the Three Minute condition should have resulted in the most convergence. Table 33 indicates support for the predictions. It might be noted that the means are the absolute discrepancy between the two alternatives in scale points.

Although the data are strong and entirely supportive of the ideas, Linder et al. (1971) have suggested that there is a slight flaw in the design of the Linder-Crane study. Since the amount of time remaining until the decision was confounded with the amount of information the subject could reasonably expect to receive about the two interviewers, the interpretation in terms of the effect of proximity *per se* should possibly be qualified. Accordingly, Linder et al. (1971) performed a very similar experiment in which amount of expected information was held constant. As evidenced by Table 34, the results are directly supportive of the first finding.

Girard (1969) conducted a study in much the same vein as the previous two. However, his strength-of-threat manipulation can be conceptualized two ways: as proximity to decision, and in terms of the behavioral implications of the preference. This will become apparent from the procedure.

TABLE 33

MEAN CONVERGENCE SCORES
(DATA FROM LINDER & CRANE, 1970)

	Time to decision	
Fifteen minutes	Eight minutes	Three minutes
12.18	9.00	6.09

TABLE 34
MEAN CONVERGENCE SCORES
(DATA FROM LINDER ET AL., 1971)

Time to decision	
Ten minutes	Three minutes
12.8	7.4

The experiment was conducted with school boys between nine and eleven years old in Turin, Italy. The choice alternatives were taken from 10 colored cards, each depicting a different kind of butterfly. The experiment had three different phases.

Phase 1. The subject was asked to rate each card on an 11-point scale of attractiveness. Once this was accomplished the experimenter decided on the decision alternatives. Each alternative was composed of a *pair* of cards.

Phase 2. Girard called this phase the "provisional choice." The experimenter identified the decision alternatives, told the subject of a forthcoming choice between them later, and then asked the subject to rank-order all 10 cards.

Phase 3. At this point the experimental conditions diverged. In the Ranking condition the subject was asked for an additional rank-ordering of the items, with the understanding that he could change the ranks or keep them the same, depending on his current preferences. In the Choice condition the subject was asked to proceed to choose one of the two pairs of cards.

The major dependent variable was the consistency or inconsistency between the second and third phases. A consistent response in the Ranking condition would mean that the relative positions of the alternatives did not change between the second (Phase 2) and third rankings, and similarly, in the Choice condition consistency was defined by the subject's choice being consistent with his Phase 2 ranking. The results showed more inconsistency in the Choice condition (see Table 35). Forty per cent of the Choice subjects showed inversions, compared against only 17% for the Ranking condition ($p < .05$).

One explanation offered by Girard for his results is consistent with the preceding discussion of temporal processes. A threat to decision freedom increases as the potential loss of freedom (commitment) approaches. In the

TABLE 35
PERCENTAGES OF SUBJECTS
SHOWING INVERSIONS

Condition	Percent
Ranking	17%
Choice	40%

condition where the person has decided, the time until decision is zero, and 40% of these subjects showed reversals. But in the other condition, some time remained until the decision; thus, the threat value of a stated preference was not as great, and only 17% of the subjects showed reversals.

There is a second and slightly different interpretation. The actual choice obviously has more behavioral implications than the re-ranking and therefore constitutes a greater threat. For this reason and for the foregoing reason, Girard's results would be anticipated on the basis of reactance theory.

Summary

The results of these three experiments suggest that freedom will be safeguarded during the decision process by means of converging the rated attractiveness of the options. The experiments, especially the first two, also give strong support to the reasoning that self-imposed threat to freedom increases as the point of decision comes closer.

Among the other theories considered, Miller's is the only one that appears to apply directly to the obtained results. If it may be assumed that an avoidance gradient was created in each study, it does seem to follow that subjects would become progressively more conflicted among the alternatives as time of decision progresses. In his language, the avoidance gradient should rise more quickly than the approach gradient. In applying Miller's notion the earlier reservations should be kept in mind.

Dissonance theory simply does not apply, for decision proximity has no counterpart in the theory. Finally, the choice-certainty principle of Mills does not operate as expected in the context of these experiments. Attempts at choice-certainty should have led to more *divergence* of the alternatives, rather than convergence.

Freedom

In previous chapters freedom was defined operationally either in terms of the choice-no-choice distinction, or in terms of whether or not subjects were aware of the choice alternatives. This section on freedom provides some continuity. In the first experiment to be described (Festinger and Walster, reported in Festinger, 1964) the variable is whether or not subjects realized which of several items were decision alternatives. The subsequent two experiments employ the more often used choice-no-choice tactic.

In all three of the present experiments the primary variable is freedom, and just one measure of convergence (or preference reversal) is taken. It is assumed, of course, that subjects given freedom are more likely to rate the alternatives closely together, or to show a tendency toward reversal of earlier preferences.

Festinger and Walster recruited coeds for an apparent market research study. At the outset each subject was asked to *rate* 12 hair styles on the basis of their personal appeal, then each of the 12 was *ranked*, and finally the subject was to choose to have her hair done free of charge in one of the styles.

The independent variable was the point in this sequence of events at which the subject learned the identity of the two choice alternatives. In the No Prior Decision condition the subject was not informed of the specific choice alternatives until after the ranking, while in the Prior Decison condition this information was disclosed before ranking. In this latter condition the subject implicitly chose by ranking, since she was aware of the alternatives while making a public discrimination between them.

If reactance is created by a decision, whether the decision is an overt commitment, a statement of preference, or any other discrimination among viable alternatives, a tendency toward preference reversal should show up soon after. In the present experiment preference reversal was measured by the actual choice, which came just after the ranking. If the subject chose the alternative initially rated lower, she was credited with a choice inversion. Sixty-two per cent of the Prior Decision subjects showed choice inversions, while just 28 per cent of the No Prior Decision subjects inverted (see Table 36). The results are supportive of the idea that the convergence or preference-reversal phenomenon is engaged primarily among subjects who have freedom of choice.

An experiment by Brehm and Rozen (1971) is an important one in demonstrating the role of prior freedom in self-imposed threats. Since the experiment also applies to the following section on importance of freedom, it will be given somewhat more detail than others. An introductory example will aid in clarification of the reasoning behind the study.

A person is standing in a bakery contemplating which of several exotic pastries to purchase. He has given several minutes to his contemplations, and

TABLE 36

PERCENTAGES OF SUBJECTS
SHOWING CHOICE INVERSIONS

Condition	Per cent
No prior decision	28%
Prior decision	62%

although he has not come to a firm decision, he has some preferences. Suddenly the baker opens the display case and introduces a new alternative—an attractive and enticing French pastry. What happens to the attractiveness of the other pastries?

The new pastry will exert a strong pull away from the other alternatives, and in this sense it acts as a barrier to choosing them. But the barrier is of a much different variety from the external physical type, for in this instance the barrier is nothing more than the person's own preference. The stronger the preference for this added item, the stronger the threat to freedom of choice among pre-existing items. This should mean that a recently-introduced attractive alternative will cause the attractiveness of old alternatives to increase, unless the new one is so superior that it completely diminishes the relative importance of the others. Further, the more important is the freedom to choose those earlier-considered pastries, the more they will gain in attractiveness due to the barrier. Based on this reasoning Brehm and Rozen conducted their experiment.

This experiment stands out from all other reactance-theory tests reported thus far because of the attempt to impart a feeling of freedom to the subjects. Not only was a choice-no-choice manipulation employed, but subjects were given considerable experience in exercising the freedom before the manipulation was introduced.

Female undergraduates were recruited for a six-session study involving consumer research. When the subject arrived for Session I she was shown three exotic Argentinian desserts. It was explained that two ratings of each item were needed: first an appearance rating, then a rating of taste. (The taste rating was not included as a dependent measure, but only to justify aspects of the procedure.) Following the two types of ratings the subject was dismissed and scheduled to return for five additional sessions.

Beginning with Session II the number of tastings was reduced by two. Subjects again rated the items for appearance, but just *one* was to be tasted and rated for taste. To vary freedom of choice some subjects found that they would be able to choose which item to taste, both in Session II and in subsequent sessions (High Freedom condition), while the Low Freedom subjects were told that they would be assigned an item to taste in each session. The same three Argentinian desserts were used in all six sessions, and consistent with the experimenter's instructions, High Freedom subjects selected an item to taste in each session while Low Freedom subjects were assigned an item.

When the subject arrived for Session VI she found a fourth item on the table, quite distinct from the Argentinian desserts. It was either a piece of pound cake or cherry cheese cake. Pound cake vs. cherry cheese was intended to be a manipulation of attractiveness of the new alternative, but since there was no significant difference in ratings of the two items they will not be discussed separately from here on. The experimenter indicated that she had been asked to add a fourth item to the array, but otherwise the procedure was to be just as before.

To review the previous theoretical thinking, an important freedom is threatened by the new item to the degree that an old item is attractive. Therefore, any tendency toward increased attractiveness of old items in the High Freedom condition should be positively related to the initial attractiveness of the item; but this relationship should not necessarily hold in the Low Freedom condition, where reactance processes would not operate.

TABLE 37

CHANGES IN ATTRACTIVENESS OF OLD ITEMS AFTER
INTRODUCTION OF A NEW ALTERNATIVE

Freedom	Attractiveness of old alternative		
	Most attractive	Middle	Least attractive
Low Freedom	−1.96	−.71	−.08
High Freedom	.33	−.26	−.74
difference	2.29	.45	−.66

As shown in Table 37 there was decreased attractiveness for the old items in all but the High Freedom–Most Attractive condition, which was the condition where the greatest reactance was expected. In examining the Low Freedom condition it appears that there was a general tendency resembling regression toward the mean, in addition to a tendency toward decreased attractiveness overall. Decrease was more prevalent among the more attractive alternatives in the Low Freedom condition. With the Low Freedom condition as a baseline for change, reactance effects are as predicted in the High Freedom condition and are more apparent when the High-Low Freedom difference is calculated. There is a substantial difference between the High and Low Freedom conditions for the Most Attractive alternative, in addition to an interaction between High-Low Freedom and Most-Least Attractive. The data are entirely consistent with the expectation that more reactance is aroused when the freedom to choose an attractive alternative is threatened.

The theoretical argument behind the importance-of-freedom variable should be reviewed in order to anticipate the next section of this chapter. When a new and appealing alternative is introduced the subject will have some desire to choose it, but to the degree he does, freedom to select old alternatives is threatened. This self-imposed threat, based in the person's desire for that new alternative, should be expected only as long as the new item is attractive enough to challenge those already under consideration. In the present experiment that prerequisite was met: The mean rating of the new alternative was approximately 18, about five points above the mean for the Most Attractive dessert. Had the new item in the present experiment been less appealing, the same effects presumably would not have been found.

Brehm, Jones, and Smith designed an experiment that demonstrates that the highest-rated alternative of an array will suffer in rating if it becomes a choice alternative. It should be evident by now that this is simply one kind of convergence, resulting from the preferred item creating a threat to the freedom to select other items. Three experiments were run, but since the procedures were similar they will be combined in the following discussion. A central aspect of this experiment is the choice–no-choice variation, which was a within-subjects variable.

Groups of undergraduates were told that ratings of books were needed. Each subject was given two lists of books, 10 books in each, and then one list was designated as a "choice" list in that the subject found he would be able to select a book from this list later. The other list was a "no choice" list, from which no book could be chosen. Certain precautions were taken against subjects choosing a book before the rating was obtained, such as warning them not to decide until the examination of books and the second rating were completed. Of course there never was any examination or second rating.

The analysis of data used the ratings in the no-choice list as a baseline. Since the list of books designated as "choice" for some subjects was used as the

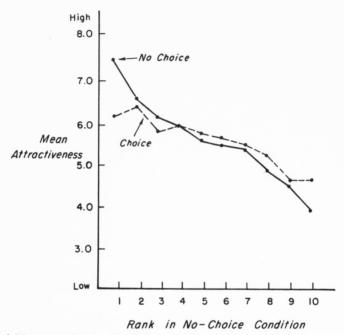

Fig. 8. Mean attractiveness of books in choice and no-choice conditions for three experiments combined.

"no choice" list for the other half of the subjects, and vice versa, it was possible to compare directly the ratings between the two conditions. Specifically, the mean ratings of each book were computed for the no-choice list. Suppose the item with the highest mean rating in the no-choice list was *The True Believer*. (Keep in mind that just half of the subjects had *The True Believer* in their no-choice list.) Then, turning to the other half of the subjects, the mean rating of *The True Believer* would be examined when it was in the choice list, and if the hypothesis holds, that rating should be lower than the comparable no-choice rating. The reasoning here is that freedom to choose other items is threatened if *The True Believer* is placed at the top of the choice list, which means there should be some tendency to reduce its rating, thereby making it more comparable to other choice books. As shown in Fig. 8, the hypothesis is supported in that the first-rated item of the no-choice list drops considerably when it is a member of the choice list ($p < .05$).[4]

[4]The results were calculated by determining the number of cases (subjects) in which an item (e.g., *The True Believer*) that was rated highest in the no-choice list dropped in rating to a point below the second-rated no-choice item when that highest-rated item was a member of the choice list. The majority of subjects (56%) showed this reversal pattern, and this percentage is significantly different from the 50% level that would be expected by chance ($p < .05$).

To encapsulate the Brehm, Jones, and Smith experiment: with a no-choice condition as a baseline, subjects given a free choice among several alternatives tended to lower their rating of the highest alternative. From the standpoint of the theory this makes good sense, for the person's attraction to the highest-rated option threatens his freedom to choose other alternatives. This reasoning applies to the Festinger-Walster and Brehm-Rozen experiments as well as to the present study.

Summary

When free and unfree subjects are compared it is only the individuals given free choice who evidence a convergence or preference-reversal phenomenon. This set of findings fits reactance theory well, but how about the other notions already examined? First, it might be noted that the choice-certainty processes described by Mills and by Janis and Mann do not seem directly evidenced here. In fact, subjects given a choice should have shown more *divergence* in ratings than subjects without a choice. There may well be circumstances under which the desire to become certain is reflected in predecisional cognitive processes, but evidence for a need to be certain is lacking thus far.

Festinger's 1964 modification of dissonance theory does appear to fit the results of this section. One of the central factors of that theory is the variable of volition. Dissonance is not aroused in the absence of volition, and certainly the three studies described in this section addressed themselves directly to the question of volition. The predecisional regret manifested in the Festinger and Walster situation was, of course, directly predicted by Festinger, and the results of the subsequent two studies also seem congruent with the analysis. Among the "free choice" subjects a statement of preference appears to produce regret.

The application of Miller's theory is less obvious. The least equivocal use of his theory is in settings in which proximity to decision is varied, for the primary focus of his thinking is on the changes in conflict due to the changing differential in gradients. But unless different positions of decision proximity are examined there is little basis for talking about changes in differential between the approach and avoidance gradients.

Importance of Freedom

There is no need to delve into specific experiments in detail, for the relevant material has already been covered. The major study of importance of freedom was by Brehm and Rozen, in which the preservation of freedom of choice centered primarily on the highest-rated of the threatened alternatives. It will be recalled that a new (fourth) alternative was introduced after several sessions, this fourth item being more attractive than either of the pre-existing three items. The subject's attraction to this novel option threatened freedom to choose all three existing items, but the importance of the freedom to choose the highest of those was, of course, greater than the importance of the freedom to choose the other two. Therefore, a tendency toward increased attractiveness was evidenced primarily for the most attractive of the three.

Importance of freedom was also relevant in the Linder and Crane study. In that experiment convergence of the two alternatives increased the closer the subject was to the decision point. However, this convergence was not distributed equally among the most preferred and least preferred alternatives. Of the two potential graduate interviewers (choice alternatives), the preferred showed little difference in rating as a function of expected time until decision, while the less preferred steadily increased in rating, creating the overall convergence effect. This differential effect can be attributed to the relative importance of accepting or rejecting the alternatives. Some detail is now in order.

In the Linder-Crane experiment the alternatives were positive, in·the sense that the freedom to accept any given alternative was more important than the freedom to reject it. When a person adopts a preference he accomplishes at least two things in the way of arousing reactance: The freedom to choose the less favored alternative is threatened, and at the same time the freedom to *reject the preferred* alternative is threatened. The relative change in ratings can be predicted by the relative importance of these two freedoms (freedom to accept the less preferred, freedom to reject the preferred). If the importance of the freedom to *reject* the preferred is the more dominant freedom, reactance will be manifested in terms of changes *downward* in that alternative. Of course such was not the case in the research reported above, and because the freedom to reject an attractive interviewer was fairly unimportant, there was not much downward shift. However, the freedom to choose the less preferred alternative was important in those studies, which means that reactance was created with respect to the loss of that freedom, and consequently the upward shift resulted.

Although this analysis is somewhat tentative, it does correspond adequately with the Linder and Crane effects. Further, the experiment by Wicklund (1970) using an external threat in the form of a fee found a similar result. A more direct experimental test of the idea would consist of varying the attractiveness of decision alternatives between the extremes of attractiveness and unattractiveness, with the expectation that regret (preference reversal) would be evidenced by decreasing preference for the highest rated alternative, given that it is undesirable. In contrast, if the decision alternatives are generally attractive, regret should take the form found in the research reported, where the less attractive option increases and the most attractive changes only slightly.

A Closer Look at Dissonance Theory
in the Context of Postdecision Regret

Of the four alternative theories introduced in this section, Festinger's analysis of regret has thus far received the best support. Miller's notion applies only to those cases in which decision proximity is varied, and even then, there are serious problems in applying his theory at all in this context. The earlier remarks in the context of the detailed description of Miller's theory indicate these reservations. The third and fourth models (Mills; Janis and Mann) assume a process opposite from that suggested by reactance theory, and thus far there has been no evidence of certainty-increasing efforts by experimental subjects.

The variable of decision proximity is the only one thus far to give the dissonance analysis serious trouble. There is no formal mechanism in Festinger's approach to regret that would take into account the person's distance from the commitment point. Other than that, the model has received almost as much support as reactance theory in this chapter, and for this reason a closer examination of the dissonance approach will be instructive, in regard to its validity. Two experiments are reported here, both of which raise serious questions about the suitability of describing regret and convergence in the cognitive-dissonance language.

Walster conducted a now-classic experiment as a direct test of Festinger's model of regret (reported in Festinger, 1964). To recapitulate, Festinger (1964) proposed that a decision is followed by a temporary regret phase, to be replaced by dissonance reduction. Very simply, the sequence is *decision, regret, dissonance reduction.* The experiment is instructive as to the accuracy of this postulated chain of events.

New draftees were asked to rate the attractiveness of ten different occupational specialties, any one of which they could potentially hold for their remaining two years in the army. After the initial rating an experimenter selected out two jobs close in attractiveness, then the subject was directed to choose one of them as his occupation for the next two years. The next step was an administration of a second attractiveness measure. The time interval between decision and the second measure was varied so that one group of subjects gave their second ratings immediately after the decision, a second group responded to the measure after 4 minutes, a third group after 15 minutes, and a fourth group after 90 minutes. Using as a dependent measure the mean change in scale distance between the two alternatives, Walster found that regret (shift toward reversal in attractiveness of the two alternatives) resulted at four minutes, with dissonance reduction (spreading apart) in all other conditions (see Table 38). The regret was not significantly different from zero, but was different from the spread in the Immediate and Fifteen Minute conditions. The only statistically significant dissonance reduc-

TABLE 38

CHANGE IN DISCREPANCY OF TWO
DECISION ALTERNATIVES IN
WALSTER'S EXPERIMENT

Condition	Change in discrepancy
Immediate	.71
Four Minute	−1.34
Fifteen Minute	2.14
Ninety Minute	.31

tion was at 15 minutes. In summary, subjects stated an explicit decision, and four minutes later the decision alternatives drew together in attractiveness. The dissonance reduction which was expected to follow the regret phase appeared at 15 minutes but virtually disappeared after 90 minutes.

An Assessment of the Dissonance
Theory Account of Regret

The main similarity between the present experiment (Brehm & Wicklund, 1970) and the previous one lies in the examination of evaluative changes of decision alternatives over an interval following the decision. However, in this experiment the time of measurement was a within-subject variable, and the experimental manipulations were designed to provide a more thorough test of Festinger's explanation of regret.

According to Festinger (1964) regret is simply the manifestation of attention turned toward the less fortunate aspects (dissonant aspects) of the decision. Once these dissonant elements have been examined sufficiently, dissonance reduction becomes possible, hence the postulated sequence of regret followed by dissonance reduction.

Since Festinger's treatment of regret assumes that attention turned on the undesirable aspects of the decision is basic to regret, it should be possible to enhance regret by forcing attention onto the negative aspects of a decision. Therefore, the present experiment included a "salience" manipulation by which the dissonant features of the choice were forcibly made salient for subjects. A low-dissonance control condition was also included, but it is not vital for this discussion.

Subjects were led to believe they were taking a type of personality test and that they would be evaluated on the basis of whether or not they could choose which of two men was better qualified for a certain position. A list of several traits was furnished to aid the subject in making her choice, and in addition to the list, a picture of each man was supplied. In each case the picture reflected a negative feature of the man. The subject was shown the trait list and corresponding pictures of the men, then was asked to rate them (premeasure) prior to choosing. Immediately after the decision the salience manipulation was introduced. In the No Salience condition all information about the two men, including the picture, was removed. But in the Salience condition the picture of the chosen man remained for the subject to examine—in fact, it was placed so that the subject could hardly avoid attending to it. Finally, measures of attractiveness of the two alternatives were taken at one-minute intervals following the decision for a total of 10 minutes.

The data over the 10-minute interval were collapsed into "maximum dissonance reduction" and "maximum regret" for each subject, and these maxima were averaged within conditions. As indicated in Table 39 the mean maximum regret was greater in the No Salience than in the Salience condition, contrary to the extrapolation from dissonance theory.

TABLE 39

MEAN CHANGES FROM PRECHOICE RATINGS[a]

Minutes after choice	High dissonance – no salience[b]	High dissonance – salience[c]
1	−3.8	−1.8
2	−4.0	−1.0
3	−4.9	−0.3
4	−2.7	−1.8
5	−2.5	−1.2
6	−2.2	−1.8
7	−2.9	0.3
8	−2.7	1.2
9	−2.7	1.3
10	−3.1	1.2

[a]Mean changes are based on the rating of the chosen alternative minus the rating of the unchosen alternative.

[b]Maximum regret = −6.91 and maximum dissonance reduction = .36.

[c]Maximum regret = −4.67 and maximum dissonance reduction = 3.50.

Summary

In Walster's experiment the postdecisional period was a combination of regret and dissonance-reduction effects, although the specific order of those effects was inconsistent with Festinger's postulated regret-then-dissonance-reduction sequence. There was a strong tendency toward dissonance reduction in Walster's Immediate condition, which was significantly different from the regret that followed at four minutes. These data alone do not support the idea that regret facilitates, bolsters, or even precedes dissonance reduction. The Brehm and Wicklund experiment offers stronger evidence against the Festinger interpretation of regret. If regret results directly from the focusing of attention on dissonant elements, regret evidently should have resulted when subjects in the Brehm-Wicklund study were forced to examine the picture (sole negative trait) of the chosen alternative. But the salience of that cognition *reduced* regret, which seems to indicate the subjects were possibly reacting defensively to the dissonant information. Aside from the ultimate explanation of the data, it looks as if Festinger's explanation of preference reversal, whether postdecision regret or predecision change, is somewhat untenable.

Dissonance theory as an explanation of regret seems to be in trouble. There is a certain justice in this conclusion because the revised theory predicts two opposing effects and does not allow any particularly convincing method by which we can know when each of the two effects should rise and fall. As illustrated by Walster's experiment, not only are both effects possible following an explicit choice (consistent with the formulation), but the effects seem to crop up at unpredictable times and not always in the right order.

Does reactance theory handle postdecision regret any better? First, the theory thus far has not addressed itself to sequential reactance effects following a definite commitment. The theoretical notion simply allows that a statement of preference, especially when implying behavioral consequences, can threaten freedom and produce convergence of ratings (regret). This is what Walster found—some tendency toward regret, and of course dissonance reduction was operating against that effect and was likely to become the stronger force at some point. A more interesting case for reactance theory can be made when theoretically-relevant variables are manipulated, but the important point is that given Walster's pattern of data, reactance theory provides an interpretation of the mere occurrence of regret in a case where the complex sequence of events stipulated by dissonance principles does not seem to occur. The reactance analysis might also be extended to the Brehm and Wicklund study, simply by noting that the existence of regret can be interpreted as a reactance phenomenon. Naturally the interpretation would be stronger had theoretically-relevant variables been employed.

EXTENSIONS AND RELATED ISSUES

The existence of a self-imposed threat phenomenon is strongly suggested by the foregoing research. The results coincide quite well with the extension of reactance theory that deals with self-imposed threats. Although two other theoretical notions can be applied to the phenomenon, that application is limited either because the theories do not reach far enough or because of evidence inconsistent with them. This section is the place to ask a couple of critical questions of reactance theory, since criticism thus far has focused on alternative notions. These critical comments are set forth under the following headings: (a) What is a totally self-imposed threat? and (b) Emergence of choice-certainty effects. Finally under a third heading decisions will be characterized as one variety of loss of freedom. This latter topic is less critical than explanatory.

What is a Totally Self-Imposed Threat?

Although the greater part of this chapter has been addressed to the effects of "self-imposed threats," it is conceivable that these effects were due in part to a discrete form of external threat. It was argued that the subject's preferences brought about a self-imposed threat to freedom. However, when such preferences became public, as was true in virtually every case, the subject may have experienced pressures from those around him to be consistent with his preferences. The research on the high pressure salesman (Wicklund et al., 1970) reported in Chapter 6 assumed this very process. It is as though the experimenter tells the subject, "If you like this one, you had better choose it." From this line of reasoning the effects in the Festinger and Walster experiment, for example, might be explained in this way: Half of the subjects ranked the alternatives with the knowledge of which two would be decision alternatives. Immediately upon giving those public rankings (in the presence of the experimenter), subjects might have felt some external pressure to make their subsequent choices consistent with the rankings. Accordingly, it could have been the felt social pressure, emanating from the experimenter's presence, that aroused reactance and generated the 62% reversals.

To state the case more generally, when a subject indicates an overt preference prior to a decision, he may experience pressure from those around him to choose consistently with the ranking. This social pressure, rather than self-imposed threats, can be viewed as the basis of convergence. This issue is even more salient in the following experiment by Rozen (1970), in which the experimenter seizes on the subject's behavior in order to predict for him his future behaviors.

Subjects were recuited for two sessions. First they took a detailed personality test, and when they returned for the second session they were asked to choose their favorite geometric design from each of several pairs of geometric designs. Just before the "critical" pair of designs was presented, the subject learned that the previously-taken personality test could be used by psychologists to predict his design-choosing behavior. The procedure was arranged so that the subject expected to be told the prediction for his choice of designs on a critical trial.

When a person learns that a personality test can predict his future behaviors, reactance should be created. It is as though a limitation is placed on the subject by his own previous test answers, and in order to restore his freedom in this situation all he has to do is choose the design not predicted. Self-imposed threat is not the sole source of reactance here, as will become apparent in a moment. The experimenter did her best to add an external threat to the already existing threat.

There were two levels of a variable called "demand." In the Demand condition the experimenter said that the test had really worked, ". . . that everybody had been accurately predicted and that it was impossible not to do what had been predicted." Then she told the subject which design he was expected to select for the critical trial. In the No Demand condition there was simply a prediction without comments.

The dependent measure was whether or not subjects chose the predicted geometric design when confronted with the critical pair of designs, and Rozen's hypothesis was supported: Significantly more subjects chose the nonpredicted design in the Demand condition than in the No Demand condition.

Rozen's experiment underlines the difficulty discussed in this section. First, this seems to be a case in which a subject's behavior apparently is threatened by his previous behavior. He answers a test in a certain way, then finds that his test performance implies limitations for subsequent choice behavior. This discovery should be enough to create reactance.

Note that for this analysis to work, the observer must have access to the subject's behavior at least twice. Otherwise, his expectation of consistency would be impossible. Clearly Rozen's experiment fills this requirement, and so does the Festinger and Walster study. But not all of the experiments herein meet this stipulation. Many of the experiments employed just one measurement, such as the Brehm and Rozen experiment where just one measure was taken after introduction of the new alternative, and the Linder and Crane (1970) and Linder et al. (1971) studies where only one measure was administered. Therefore, to view all of the preceding effects as the result of social pressure would be premature. And the important point is that the existence of self-imposed threat does seem to be an adequate account of those studies not involving repeated measurements. The Brehm, Jones, and Smith study may be an extreme case of absence of social pressure. There was no direct route whereby subjects might be monitored, and further, since there were no repeated measures, the subject would in no way be concerned with appearing consistent.

Emergence of Choice-Certainty Effects

Self-imposed threats vs. predecisional divergence. The preceding analysis assumes a threat to freedom when one manifests a clear discrimination among alternatives. To the degree that such discrimination is performed explicitly, the individual should feel a threat to his freedom to choose lower-ranked alternatives. Publicity will add to the reactance effects, such that the possible public observation of an overt discrimination should heighten the reactance that has been created by a self-imposed threat. It has already been noted that choice-certainty effects seem to be nonexistent, or at least shrouded, given the procedures of the several experiments reviewed here. However, there is one method that could be employed to lower the reactance-arousing potential of the decision-making process, while at the same time giving the choice-certainty phenomenon a chance to operate. Such a method was employed by O'Neal and Mills (1969), although not for the express purpose of minimizing reactance.

The requirements for a reactance-minimizing decision-making procedure are these: Let the subject contemplate and rate the alternatives without his being particularly aware of discriminating among them. O'Neal and Mills showed male subjects 16 photographs of girls, some of whom were supposedly promiscuous. The experimenter pointed out eight of the pictures, and told the subject that in a second study he would be asked to decide which of the eight were pictures of promiscuous girls. These pictures, therefore, can be called "decision" pictures, while the remaining eight were "nondecision" pictures. The subject then proceeded to rank the 16 photographs on each of eight traits, such as "artistic" and "sincere."

How does this procedure minimize reactance? Since subjects were given the "decision" and "nondecision" pictures all together, and since rankings were performed on eight different dimensions, any possible discrimination between choice alternatives would have tended to become blurred. It was not as though the subject could indicate a bold, blatant, discrimination as in the research earlier reported, for there was a good deal of confusion possible. In the presence of this confusion, and in the absence of clear, single-dimension discriminations, self-imposed threats to freedom certainly should have been reduced. Also tending to minimize reactance was the fact that no decision was expected until a later date.

If reactance was minimized, the choice-certainty processes should have been manifested in the following way: When a girl receives a high ranking on

Trait A, she should also tend to receive a high ranking on the other seven traits, thus manifesting the subject's desire to enter into the decision with a clear orientation. This consistency among rankings was evaluated by computing the intercorrelations among traits, and consistent with the choice-certainty hypothesis, the intercorrelation was higher for "decision" pictures than for "nondecision" pictures. Accordingly, it does appear as if choice-certainty effects, which run contrary to reactance phenomena, can appear when conditions for self-imposed threat are minimal. It might be added that O'Neal (1971) found a similar choice-certainty phenomenon, and that importance of the anticipated choice exaggerated the effect.

Guesswork: selective exposure. Assuming a propensity to avoid both reactance arousal and stimuli that bring forth reactance, there is some possibility that an individual would attempt to bring certain kinds of information into his focus during the decision process. The first idea that comes to mind is a selective-exposure process paralleling the convergence effects shown in self-imposed threat research. Information would be read, absorbed, and sought after, provided that it convinces the person of his freedom. In more molecular terms, information favoring the less-preferred alternative should be preferred over that favoring the preferred alternative, until a point is reached where the alternatives become approximately equal in attractiveness.

There are three weaknesses in the argument suggesting that reactance (or anticipated reactance) can result in selective exposure. One of these is that evidence by Mills (1965) seems to indicate that selective exposure takes a form just opposite from that suggested in the preceding paragraph, and second, the argument assumes that reactance can be anticipated and the reactance-arousing events avoided. The first difficulty is not a major one, for it is possible that reactance and choice-certainty processes can co-exist, but under somewhat different circumstances. The second difficulty is problematic only in the sense that we don't yet know if the concepts of "anticipation" and "avoidance" apply to reactance as a motivational state. Third, exposure to information does not entail a commitment to alternatives, nor is a commitment even strongly implied; thus, the relevance of exposure to reactance arousal may be minimal.

The Theoretical Role of Decision: Loss of Expectation of Freedom

Figure 9, an extrapolation from the previous experiments, suggests two distinct processes: freedom-restoring phenomena that are reflected in a convergence of alternatives, or change of preference, as opposed to dissonance reduction, uncertainty reduction, or rationalization. It has been argued that the decision is an arbitrary point selected by the observer, beyond which dissonance-reduction processes are supposed to be realized. Although the present chapter has treated the subject's statement of decision as something psychologically real and qualitatively distinct from other discriminations among alternatives, we have as yet to find any good reason why an explicit decision should create effects qualitatively different from less explicit decisions and statements of preference. And the question remains, how are we to interpret the findings depicted in Fig. 9? In short, why do the effects of reactance appear to be outweighed by dissonance reduction or uncertainty reduction once there is an overt commitment?

Although there is as yet no research describing the precise antecedents of the person's expectations about whether or not he is free to act, it seems plausible that reactance would cease to operate at some point after the freedom has been totally eliminated. And during the course of a decision it is likely that an irreversible commitment would act as an elimination, as has been suggested earlier. This is not to say that it takes a public statement on the part of the decision-maker before his freedom is lost, for at any time during the sequence he may impart such a strong direction to his activities that he no longer has a sense of different possibilities. But it would not be far wrong to suggest that this self-imposed loss coincides approximately with a public statement, since it would be the act of announcing the decision to others that renders difficult a reversal of the action. What chain of events is set in motion once the freedom has been usurped? Initially there should be reactance arousal, followed by the adaptation to lack of freedom. Therefore, reactance effects will dissipate as the person develops an expectancy of no freedom.

From the preceding reasoning it follows that the dissonance reduction or choice-certainty effects, which are equivalent, would come to dominate as soon as the person no longer expects freedom, for the effects of reactance would cease to interfere with the attainment of certainty, rationalization, or dissonance reduction. The person is no longer motivated to preserve the

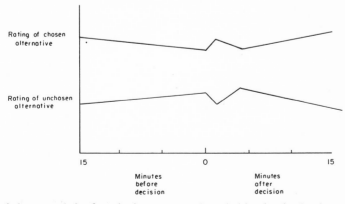

Fig. 9. An extrapolation from the data on pre- and postdecisional evaluative changes.

viability of his former options, and in the absence of those forces the person will justify his preferred or chosen course of action.

Although Fig. 9 would suggest that reactance processes overpower other effects until some point after the loss of freedom, such a relationship is not necessary. A predecisional spreading apart of the alternatives would not be surprising and may be found when reactance-arousing elements are minimal. The important point for the present is simply that an irreversible commitment does make a substantial psychological difference, the reason being that reactance effects should cease at some point following the loss of freedom.

17
ADDITIONAL MEANINGS OF FREEDOM AND QUESTIONS FOR REACTANCE THEORY

ADDITIONAL MEANINGS OF FREEDOM

This chapter will begin by considering two other psychologists' concepts of freedom. As will be seen these other definitions of freedom are at variance from what has been studied in this volume, and it is interesting to note how reactance theory would change if those notions of freedom were to be inserted into reactance theory.

B. F. Skinner

Skinner's definition of freedom differs in two respects from the definition we have assumed thus far. Loss of freedom in Skinner's language is equated with encountering aversive stimulation, and the idea of personal control does not appear in his system. A person is free when he removes himself *or* is removed from aversive situations.

In 1971 Skinner created some turbulence in popular psychology through his treatise on freedom and dignity. The central idea can be condensed into a notion of attribution of causality. Skinner would abandon the use of such terms as "honor," "dignity," "morality," and "freedom" in deference to the external factors controlling behavior. As analyzed by Skinner "freedom" becomes identical with the absence of aversive control. He proposes that "the literature" of freedom has focused almost exclusively on the virtue of avoidance of aversive stimulation, and that it seldom invokes the notion of freedom in the context of control by positive reinforcement. In short, Skinner's "freedom" cannot be equated with the absence of control, but instead is synonymous with avoidance of negative consequences. The Skinnerian position can be summed up by the following quote from *Beyond Freedom and Dignity:*

> Man's struggle for freedom is not due to a will to be free, but to certain behavioral processes characteristic of the human organism, the chief effect of which is the avoidance of or escape from so-called "aversive" features of the environment [p. 42].

Evidently Skinner's model of the free man is a severe departure from the model implicit in reactance ideas. According to the Skinnerian conception the organism's freedom would not be altered significantly by an imposed increase or decrease in choice, as in previously-discussed experiments. Moreover, since giving a person something he wants anyway (cf. some of the barrier research) would not involve aversive consequences, Skinner's "freedom" would be unaffected by such a manipulation.

The Skinnerian-reactance contrast seems clear: Reactance theory views the person as desiring to manage his own destiny and remain independent, even if doing so means inflicting on himself outcomes that are less than totally favorable. But Skinner's free man does not seem concerned with avoiding the status of a dependent pawn; the focal consideration is intake of the most positive outcomes.

Steiner

One of the most systematic discussions of the concept "freedom" is found in a recent attempt at integration by Steiner (1970) on perceived freedom. The first of two types of freedom dealt with is called "outcome freedom," which is synonymous with the possibility of goal attainment. If a person perceives that desired outcomes are available he experiences outcome freedom. There is a notable resemblance to Skinner's definition. If Steiner's definition of freedom is inserted into reactance theory, "frustration" then becomes the essence of the theory. Obviously frustration of goal-oriented responses does not capture the richness of reactance theory and its associated phenomena. When a third-ranked decision alternative increases in value due to its elimination we need more than the concept of frustration for explanation.

The important type of freedom for this volume is called "decision freedom" by Steiner. Decision freedom operates relatively independently of outcome freedom and is viewed by Steiner as the free person's comparison of the relative magnitudes of alternative outcomes. A person can have high "decision freedom" even when the alternatives in question are somewhat unattractive, that is, when outcome freedom is minimal. The existence of decision freedom is, for Steiner, strictly a function of the discrepancy between the goodness of alternative outcomes. The more equal are various alternative gains, the more a person has decision freedom.

Steiner's "decision freedom" appears to equate freedom with conflict, and in applying this version of decision freedom to reactance theory some interesting implications appear. (a) If a person is free when there is maximal conflict between choice alternatives, what happens to the importance of this freedom when the alternatives overlap in function? It is not clear that Steiner employs the *discriminability* or *differential utility* of decision alternatives as criteria of freedom, which means that a person has a free choice even when the alternatives are virtually identical in quality or function. (*b*) Alternative gains may be seen as equally attractive because the person is incapable of making fine distinctions. Apparently then, a decision freedom could arise from the circumstance that a person knows nothing about the alternatives and cannot draw important discriminations as a basis for his behaviors. Both of these implications are in contrast to the theory and research on competence and importance of decision freedom discussed earlier; however, there is as yet no research bearing directly on the question of whether or not conflict increases reactance. Reactance theory does not necessarily treat conflict as an antecedent of important freedoms, and when Steiner's definition of decision freedom is substituted for the one represented earlier in this writing some provocative and testable contrasts appear.

QUESTIONS FOR THE THEORY
Free Will

At some point in a discussion of freedom the issue of determinism vs. indeterminism is inevitable (i.e., determined). The issue is not vital in the context of reactance theory and will be dispensed with quickly. There is no contradiction in presuming that the *feeling* of free will, which is basic to the theory, is in actuality determined. And ironically, it is more sound theoretically to assume the position of the determinist, for if the person's reaction to threatened freedom is not determined by antecedent events the theory is hardly of any value. Although the free-will issue does not in itself have grave implications for the theory, the issue does lead into a consideration of the precise nature of freedom, which is touched upon next.

Reactance Arousal: Response to Internal Forces?

As the theory is stated and has been interpreted, there is a division between internal and external forces. The internal forces can be described as the person's preferences, motivations, habits, or drive states; and the freedoms are defined through the existence of those forces together with the existence of several possible directions in which those forces can move. The external forces consist of that which has causality outside the person's personal control, and empirically, the conditions used to create reactance have been physical or social elements clearly out of the realm of the subject's personal control. If a person's direction is under the control of his own volition, motivation, or habit, his behavior can often be characterized as free; but when some aspect of himself or his situation becomes controlled by forces outside himself, that aspect is thereby subject to limitation of freedom. A few examples might elucidate the external-internal distinction.

A young man has the options of becoming either a butcher or a mortician. He is far from making a decision and is at a point where he wants to explore each possibility in depth. Accordingly, he takes whatever steps are instrumental in familiarizing himself with each vocation, and when a part-time job as the local mortician's helper opens up he decides to take the position. Of course this commitment does not obligate him to become a mortician. According to the usual interpretation of reactance theory the young man remains in a predecisional state and is exercising his freedom to become more familiar with the choice alternatives. In fact, he is increasing his competence as a decision-maker. To increase his competence he increases his personal control over the situation; thus, by exposing himself to relevant information he is making his freedom more important.

Contrasting the setting described above with one in which the person is *forced* by someone else to take an apprenticeship in a mortuary, we should find all of the reactance in the second situation. The person's direction is imparted by forces other than those residing in his volition, opinions, or habits, and he should resist these external forces in whatever way is prescribed by the theory.

But already there are exceptions to this strict internal-external dichotomy. Linder and Crane (1970), Linder et al. (1971), and Wicklund (1970) have proposed a notion of "self-imposed threat to freedom" (Chapter 16). The idea is simply that a person in the predecisional state threatens his own freedom by adopting preferences. Even though the preference is an internally-located event, presumably initiated with the guide of volition, the preference statement appears to threaten the freedom to choose other alternatives, and more so if the decision point is close at hand.

The question of "what is freedom" should be pursued more thoroughly in the context of the internal-external causality issue. One approach to the determinism-indeterminism issue has been that behavior can be *determined* by the individual's own motives, independent of whether or not his behaviors are determined by external influences. Drawing an analogy to reactance theory, what are the effects of assuming that the individual might feel "constrained," "impelled," "determined," or "threatened" by internal forces? First, it will be important to elaborate on the nature of these internal forces, and a rough list such as the following includes some of the important ones:

hereditary-genetic
physical characteristics
biological and other motives
habits and personal customs
attitudes
emotional states

Many of these internal influences take effect without volitional mediation, so it may be important to qualify the distinction between internal and external forces. In terms of the theoretical comments in the preceding chapters, only those forces over which the individual has control should be treated as "internal." Reexamining the dichotomy, reactance can be created by genetic and physical factors, possibly by habits of the nature of uncontrollable obsessions, and of course by events external to the person. That is, the uncontrollable internal factors that are not subject to volition could be reactance arousing factors. In contrast, those influences that originate in volition, where there are feelings of control, will not arouse reactance but instead will constitute the exercise of free behavior. But looking back at the research and associated theoretical arguments of the self-imposed-threat chapter, is this a sensible dichotomy? Certainly a preference for a decision alternative is a matter of volition as far as the subject is concerned, yet this preference was viewed by the above authors as a self-imposed threat.

In what sense could a person's behavior be *determined* by his own volition? When someone is confronted with a choice situation he may have varying degrees of control over the situation, depending on the state of his relevant knowledge. It is possible to approach a decision in a state of total ignorance, or in a state of complete knowledge. Both individuals, the ignorant and the knowledgable, are seen as acting out of volition when they make the decision, and both can be depended upon to say they acted freely. But was the knowledgable person's decision *determined* by his knowledge? And if so, did this person exercise as much volition as did the ignorant decision-maker?

Such considerations point to an alternative definition of freedom, in some ways opposed to that set forth thus far. The totally free person may be one who is free from all constraints, whether those constraints arise from within or without, and one who is free to oscillate and hover between courses of action without feeling any impelling forces. It is an interesting possibility that such an individual would under some circumstances prefer the state of ignorance, for any internal direction and motivation arising from knowledge or other biases would reduce the totally free state.

This alternative conception of freedom does not fit readily into pre-existing reactance theory, for the research has been based on an assumption that a person who is knowledgable, competent, and who carries strong preferences will be the ideal reactance subject. The running theoretical definition does not presuppose freedom from internal constraint and direction, but on the contrary, assumes that strong internal forces are a precondition for resistance to external forces. And in the context of self-imposed threats it must likewise be assumed that strong internal forces are a precondition for resistance to *other* internal forces.

Since it has already been shown that a competent person (i.e., one governed strongly by internal forces) is more subject to reactance arousal, it would be futile as well as contradictory to attempt to replace the original reactance-theory conception with a notion that says that freedom is the absence of all controlling external *and* internal forces. However, the interesting possibility concerns the individual who is not yet competent, nor internally directed in any manner. Perhaps he would prefer that totally free state to one in which he has internal direction. As yet there is no definite empirical answer to the question, although there are some hints of an answer in the research by Rathjen, below.

When Is Freedom Avoided or Sought?

The most obvious answer to this question comes from Erich Fromm's *Escape from Freedom* (1941). Human growth is conceptualized by Fromm as possessing a dual character. As human reason, power, strength and integration develop, the human acquires more freedom but at the same time incurs increased threats of isolation. With these feelings of individuation or isolation come questions concerning one's meaning in the world and a concern about powerlessness and insignificance as an individual. There is already theoretical and empirical reason to suppose that the person who realizes himself as a separate identity suffers unhappiness (Duval & Wicklund, 1972; Hoffer, 1951; Ickes, Wicklund, & Ferris, 1973; Zimbardo, 1969), but the interesting implication of Fromm's ideas lies in his suggestion that freedom from external constraints is tantamount to the feeling of being separated or individuated.

Fromm proceeds to exemplify his thesis through such examples as the Nazis acquiring members by virtue of the individual German citizen's revulsion at the feeling of loneliness that comes out of freedom. There is no advantage at present in offering further examples, since the central point is simply that freedom can breed the individuated, hence unhappy individual. The precise conditions under which freedom has such an effect might better be established by means of research; for the present we will leave Fromm's thesis as an interesting possibility.

Among experimental studies that relate to the escape from freedom, three stand out as directly bearing on the issue. Studies by Kiesler (1966) and Hendrick, Mills, and Kiesler (1968) indicate that the time taken to contemplate a decision is sometimes less when alternatives are difficult to discriminate from one another. Perhaps this finding can be reduced to the idea that people avoid conflict, and when a decision is difficult the exercise of freedom is short-circuited in the service of quickly eliminating conflict.

A result by Braden and Walster, reported in Festinger (1964), is conceptually similar. A situation was arranged in which subjects were told they could receive either of two phonograph records. The method by which the records were given to subjects was left up to the individual subject, such that the person could either choose among the two records or receive one by a flip of the coin. In the Anticipated Dissonance condition subjects were told they would have to give a recommendation of the record they did not receive, while Anticipated Consonance subjects found that the recommendation was to be consistent with the choice. As expected, the frequency of preference for the coin-flip procedure was greater among Anticipated Dissonance subjects, with most of them foregoing the choice. The foregoing of freedom in this experiment was more dramatic than in the decision-time experiments. Subjects actually refused to decide in the face of conflict. It seems entirely reasonable that a person would not want the responsibility for a decision that would make him look foolish, and it was apparently this source of conflict that brought subjects to completely abdicate this freedom.

To speculate, it is possible that the exercise of freedoms is an appealing endeavor as long as the exercise does not preclude further exercise of the same freedoms. The paradoxical aspect of "exercise of freedom" is that the phrase often stands for the elimination, by decision, of that freedom. But how do we bestow upon someone a freedom that does not carry the responsibility for choice, or for self-imposed elimination of that freedom? Perhaps the reluctance of people to seek out freedom is not surprising when the acquisition of a freedom is tantamount to voluntarily destroying it at some future time.

Reactance theory and the other theories considered earlier have not dealt directly with questions bearing on the acquisition of freedom. Instead the focus has been on the defense of freedom once acquired. The evidence indicates that existing freedoms are highly valued and defensively protected, but the psychology of the not-yet-free person remains to be understood. One pioneering investigation of this matter was undertaken by Rathjen (1972). Just the relevant aspects of her dissertation experiment will be discussed.

Male subjects were recruited for a study of taste and found that they were obliged to drink six ounces of an unpleasant solution named "Catan." Further, the subject found that his unpleasant experience might not be as bad as anticipated, for the experimenter went on to describe some taste enhancers being tested. It was said that taste enhancers generally have the quality of improving the taste of anything consumed and that several of these enhancers were being tested in the experiment. The experimenter noted that not all of the enhancers being tried are effective: Some make food unpleasant and bitter rather than tasty.

The experimenter went on to set the stage for the subject to acquire freedom. She said that normally the enhancers are given to subjects randomly, meaning that any given subject might wind up with an effective or ineffective taste enhancer. However, the subject was informed that he could exercise a free choice among the enhancers as long as he was willing to drink large (but unspecified) quantities of Catan. He was told to indicate how much Catan he would be willing to drink, with the understanding that if he committed himself to a large enough quantity he would then have the freedom to choose. Note that the amount of Catan one is willing to drink is a reasonable behavioral measure of desire for freedom. *Really?*

The freedom to be acquired had different qualities, depending on experimental condition. Subjects in the Certain condition were told that their potential free choice would carry with it knowledge of which enhancers are effective, while subjects in the Uncertain condition were to remain ignorant of the enhancer effectiveness if they acquired the freedom to choose. Subjects in the High Importance condition were told the enhancer would last 24 hours; Low Importance subjects were told it would last one hour.

The certainty manipulation had an effect consistent with common sense. Subjects who expected to be certain (i.e., to know which enhancer is effective) indicated a high desire for freedom of choice by pledging themselves to high quantities of Catan, but Uncertain subjects were reluctant to enter into the choice. The importance variable also came out as Rathjen predicted, with High Importance subjects desiring more freedom of choice than Low Importance subjects.

An important conclusion from Rathjen's data concerns the parallel between the processes of acquiring freedom and having an existing freedom threatened. In the case of an existing freedom, reactance is created when the freedom is important and when the subject is competent. Rathjen found a desire for freedom under those same conditions, suggesting that all of the theoretical structure examined to this point may apply in a parallel fashion to the person without freedom who struggles to obtain it. The parallel is incomplete, but this experiment leads to an optimism about extending the central ideas of reactance theory.

poor concluding section

REFERENCES

Abelson, R.P., & Miller, J.C. Negative persuasion via personal insult. *Journal of Experimental Social Psychology*, 1967, **3**, 321-333.

Abelson, R. P., & Rosenberg, M. J. Symbolic psycho-logic: A model of attitudinal cognition. *Behavioral Science*, 1958, **3**, 1-13.

Adams, D. K. Restatement of the problem of learning. *British Journal of Psychology*, 1931, **22**, 150-178.

Albert, S., & Dabbs, J. M. Physical distance and persuasion. *Journal of Personality and Social Psychology*, 1970, **15**, 265-270.

Allyn, J., & Festinger, L. The effectiveness of unanticipated persuasive communications. *Journal of Abnormal and Social Psychology*, 1961, **62**, 35-40.

Aronson, E. The effect of effort on the attractiveness of rewarded and unrewarded stimuli. *Journal of Abnormal and Social Psychology*, 1961, **63**, 375-380.

Aronson, E., & Mills, J. The effect of severity of initiation on liking for a group. *Journal of Abnormal and Social Psychology*, 1959, **59**, 177-181.

Ashmore, R. D., Ramchandra, V., & Jones, R. A. Censorship as an attitude change induction. Paper presented at the meeting of the Eastern Psychological Association, New York, April, 1971.

Back, K. W. Influence through social communication. *Journal of Abnormal and Social Psychology*, 1951, **46**, 9-23.

Bateson, G. The frustration-aggression hypothesis and culture. *Psychological Review*, 1941, **48**, 350-355.

Berkowitz, L. *Aggression: A social psychological analysis*. New York: McGraw-Hill, 1962.

Berkowitz, L., & Daniels, L. R. Responsibility and dependency. *Journal of Abnormal and Social Psychology*, 1963, **66**, 429-436.

Berkowitz, L., & Daniels, L. R. Affecting the salience of the social responsibility norm: Effects of past help on the response to dependency relationships. *Journal of Abnormal and Social Psychology*, 1964, **68**, 275-281.

Berscheid, E. Opinion change and communicator-communicatee similarity and dissimilarity. *Journal of Personality and Social Psychology*, 1966, **4**, 670-680.

Berscheid, E., & Walster, E. *Interpersonal attraction*. Reading, Mass.: Addison-Wesley, 1969.

Brehm, J. W. *A theory of psychological reactance*. New York: Academic Press, 1966.

Brehm, J. W., & Cohen, A. R. Re-evaluation of choice alternatives as a function of their number and qualitative similarity. *Journal of Abnormal and Social Psychology*, 1959, **58**, 373-378.

Brehm, J. W., & Cohen, A. R. *Explorations in cognitive dissonance*. New York: Wiley, 1962.

Brehm, J. W., & Rozen, E. Attractiveness of old alternatives when a new, attractive alternative is introduced. *Journal of Personality and Social Psychology,* 1971, **20**, 261-266.

Brehm, J. W., & Sensenig, J. Social influence as a function of attempted and implied usurpation of choice. *Journal of Personality and Social Psychology,* 1966, **4**, 703-707.

Brehm, J. W., Stires, L. K., Sensenig, J., & Shaban, J. The attractiveness of an eliminated choice alternative. *Journal of Experimental Social Psychology,* 1966, **2**, 301-313.

Brehm, J. W., & Wicklund, R. A. Regret and dissonance reduction as a function of postdecision salience of dissonant information. *Journal of Personality and Social Psychology,* 1970, **14**, 1-7.

Brock, T. C. Effects of prior dishonesty on postdecision dissonance. *Journal of Abnormal and Social Psychology,* 1963, **66**, 325-331.

Brock, T. C. Communicator-recipient similarity and decision change. *Journal of Personality and Social Psychology,* 1965, **1**, 650-654.

Buss, A. *The psychology of aggression.* New York: Wiley, 1961.

Cohen, A. R. Social norms, arbitrariness of frustration, and status of the agent of frustration in the frustration-aggression hypothesis. *Journal of Abnormal and Social Psychology,* 1955, **51**, 222-226.

Cohen, A. R. Communication discrepancy and attitude change: A dissonance theory approach. *Journal of Personality,* 1959, **27**, 386-396.

Cohen, A. R. A dissonance analysis of the boomerang effect. *Journal of Personality,* 1962, **30**, 75-88.

Cooper, J., & Jones, E. E. Opinion divergence as a strategy to avoid being miscast. *Journal of Personality and Social Psychology,* 1969, **13**, 23-30.

Dean, R. B., Austin, J. A., & Watts, W. A. Forewarning effects in persuasion: Field and classroom experiments. *Journal of Personality and Social Psychology,* 1971, **18**, 210-221.

Dollard, J., Doob, L. W., Miller, N.E., Mowrer, O. H., & Sears, R.R. *Frustration and aggression.* New Haven: Yale University Press, 1939.

Doob, A. N., & Zabrack, M. The effect of freedom-threatening instructions and monetary inducement on compliance. *Canadian Journal of Behavioral Science,* 1971, **3**, 408-412.

Duval, S., & Wicklund, R.A. *A theory of objective self awareness.* New York: Academic Press, 1972.

Feather, N. T. Subjective probability and decision under uncertainty. *Psychological Review,* 1959, **66**, 150-164. (a)

Feather, N. T. Success probability and choice behavior. *Journal of Experimental Psychology,* 1959, **58**, 257-266. (b)

Festinger, L. Informal social communication. *Psychological Review,* 1950, **57**, 271-283.

Festinger, L. A theory of social comparison processes. *Human Relations,* 1954, **7,** 117-140.

Festinger, L. *A theory of cognitive dissonance.* Stanford, Calif.: Stanford University Press, 1957.

Festinger, L. *Conflict, decision, and dissonance.* Stanford, Calif.: Stanford University Press, 1964.

Festinger, L., & Maccoby, N. On resistance to persuasive communications. *Journal of Abnormal and Social Psychology,* 1964, **68,** 359-366.

Filer, R. J. Frustration, satisfaction, and other factors affecting the attractiveness of goal objects. *Journal of Abnormal and Social Psychology,* 1952, **47,** 203-212.

Fishbein, M. A consideration of beliefs, attitudes, and their relationships. In I.D. Steiner & M. Fishbein (Eds.), *Current studies in social psychology.* New York: Holt, Rinehart & Winston, 1965.

French, J. R. P., Jr., & Raven, B. The bases of social power. In D. Cartwright (Ed.), *Studies in social power.* Ann Arbor, Mich.: Institute for Social Research, 1959.

Fromm, E. *Escape from freedom.* New York: Rinehart, 1941.

Gerard, H. B., & Mathewson, G. C. The effects of severity of initiation on liking for a group: A replication. *Journal of Experimental Social Psychology,* 1966, **2,** 278-287.

Girard, G. The expression of regret in evaluation and in choice. Unpublished manuscript, Universita di Milano, 1969.

Goranson, R. E., & Berkowitz. L. Reciprocity and social responsibility reactions to prior help. *Journal of Personality and Social Psychology,* 1966, **3,** 227-232.

Grabitz-Gniech, G. Some restrictive conditions for the occurrence of psychological reactance. *Journal of Personality and Social Psychology,* 1971, **19,** 188-196.

Hammock, T., & Brehm, J. W. The attractiveness of choice alternatives when freedom to choose is eliminated by a social agent. *Journal of Personality,* 1966, **34,** 546-554.

Heider, F. *The psychology of interpersonal relations.* New York: Wiley, 1958.

Heller, J. F., Pallak, M. S., & Picek, J. M. The interactive effects of intent and threat on boomerang attitude change. *Journal of Personality and Social Psychology,* 1973, **26,** 273-279.

Hendrick, C., Mills, J., & Kiesler. C. A. Decision time as a function of the number and complexity of equally attractive alternatives. *Journal of Personality and Social Psychology,* 1968, **8,** 313-318.

Hoffer, E. *The true believer.* New York: Harper & Row, 1951.

Ickes, W. J., Wicklund, R. A., & Ferris, C. B. Objective self-awareness and self-esteem. *Journal of Experimental Social Psychology,* 1973, **9,** 202-219.

Janis, I. L. & Mann, L. A conflict-theory approach to attitude change and decision making. In A. G. Greenwald, T. C. Brock, & T. M. Ostrom (Eds.). *Psychological foundations of attitudes.* New York: Academic Press, 1968.

Jones, E. E. *Ingratiation.* New York: Appleton-Century-Crofts, 1964.

Jones, R. A. Volunteering to help: The effects of choice, dependence, and anticipated dependence. *Journal of Personality and Social Psychology,* 1970, **14,** 121-129.

Jones, R. A., & Brehm, J. W. Persuasiveness of one- and two-sided communications as a function of awareness there are two sides. *Journal of Experimental Social Psychology,* 1970, **6,** 47-56.

Katz, D. *Animals and men.* New York: Longmans, Green, 1937.

Kiesler, C. A. Conflict and number of choice alternatives. *Psychological Reports,* 1966, **18,** 603-610.

Kiesler, C. A., & Kiesler, S. B. Role of forewarning in persuasive communications. *Journal of Abnormal and Social Psychology,* 1964, **68,** 547-549.

Knott, P. D., Nunnally, J. C., & Duchnowski, A. J. Effects of frustration on primary and conditioned incentive value. *Journal of Experimental Research in Personality,* 1967, **2,** 140-149.

Kregarman, J. J., & Worchel, P. Arbitrariness of frustration and aggression. *Journal of Abnormal and Social Psychology,* 1961, **63,** 183-187.

Lawson, R. *Frustration: The development of a scientific concept.* New York: Macmillan, 1965.

Lewin, K. Defining the "field at a given time." *Psychological Review,* 1943, **50,** 292-310.

Lewin, K. Studies in group decision. In T. M. Newcomb & E. L. Hartley (Eds.), *Readings in social psychology.* New York: Holt, 1947.

Linder, D. E., Cooper, J., & Jones, E. E. Decision freedom as a determinant of the role of incentive magnitude in attitude change. *Journal of Personality and Social Psychology,* 1967, **6,** 245-254.

Linder, D. E., Cooper, J., & Wicklund, R. A. Pre-exposure persuasion as a result of commitment to pre-exposure effort. *Journal of Experimental Social Psychology,* 1968, **4,** 470-482.

Linder, D. E., & Crane, K. A. Reactance theory analysis of predecisional cognitive processes. *Journal of Personality and Social Psychology,* 1970, **15,** 258-264.

Linder, D. E., & Worchel, S. Opinion change as a result of effortfully drawing a counterattitudinal conclusion. *Journal of Experimental Social Psychology,* 1970, **6,** 432-448.

Linder, D. E., Wortman, C. B., & Brehm, J. W. Temporal changes in predecision preferences among choice alternatives. *Journal of Personality and Social Psychology,* 1971, **19,** 282-284.

Mann, L., Janis, I. L., & Chaplin, R. Effects of anticipation of forthcoming information on predecisional processes. *Journal of Personality and Social Psychology*, 1969, 11, 10-16.

Maxwell, A. E. *Analysing qualitative data*. New York: Wiley, 1961.

McGuire, W. J. Resistance to persuasion conferred by active and passive prior refutation of the same and alternative counterarguments. *Journal of Abnormal and Social Psychology*, 1961, 63, 326-332.

Miller, N. E. Experimental studies of conflict. In J. McV. Hunt (Ed.), *Personality and the behavior disorders*. Vol. 1. New York: Ronald Press, 1944.

Miller, N. E. Liberalization of basic S-R concepts: Extensions to conflict behavior, motivation, and social learning. In S. Koch (Ed.), *Psychology: The study of a science*. Vol. 2. New York: McGraw-Hill, 1959.

Mills, J. The effect of certainty on exposure to information prior to commitment. *Journal of Experimental Social Psychology*, 1965, 1, 348-355.

Mills, J. Opinion change as a function of the communicator's desire to influence and liking for the audience. *Journal of Experimental Social Psychology*, 1966, 2, 152-159.

Mills, J. Interest in supporting and discrepant information. In R. P. Abelson, E. Aronson, W. J. McGuire, T. M. Newcomb, M. J. Rosenberg, & P. H. Tannenbaum (Eds.), *Theories of cognitive consistency: A sourcebook*. Chicago: Rand McNally, 1968.

Mills, J., & Aronson, E. Opinion change as a function of the communicator's attractiveness and desire to influence. *Journal of Personality and Social Psychology*, 1965, 1, 173-177.

Mischel, W., & Masters, J. C. Effects of probability of reward attainment on responses to frustration. *Journal of Personality and Social Psychology*, 1966, 3, 390-396.

Newcomb, T. M. An approach to the study of communicative acts. *Psychological Review*, 1953, 60, 393-404.

O'Neal, E. Influence of future choice importance and arousal upon the halo effect. *Journal of Personality and Social Psychology*, 1971, 19, 334-340.

O'Neal, E., & Mills, J. The influence of anticipated choice on the halo effect. *Journal of Experimental Social Psychology*, 1969, 5, 347-351.

Osgood, C. E., & Tannenbaum, P. H. The principle of congruity in the prediction of attitude change. *Psychological Review*, 1955, 62, 42-55.

Pallak, M. S., & Heller, J. F. Interactive effects of commitment to future interaction and threat to attitudinal freedom. *Journal of Personality and Social Psychology*, 1971, 17, 325-331.

Pastore, N. A neglected factor in the frustration-aggression hypothesis: A comment. *Journal of Psychology*, 1950, 29, 271-279.

Pastore, N. The role of arbitrariness in the frustration-aggression hypothesis. *Journal of Abnormal and Social Psychology*, 1952, 47, 728-731.

Piaget, J. *Judgment and reasoning in the child.* Totowa, N.J.: Littlefield, Adams, and Co., 1966. (Originally published: London: K. Paul, Trench, Trubner, & Co., 1924.)

Rathjen, D. The influence of certainty, importance, and the number of alternatives on the desire for choice. Unpublished doctoral dissertation, University of Texas at Austin, 1972.

Rozen, E. Effects of a reactance manipulation on compliance in an experimental situation. Unpublished master's thesis, State University of New York at Stony Brook, 1970.

Schwartz, S. H. Elicitation of moral obligation and self-sacrificing behavior: An experimental study of volunteering to be a bone marrow donor. *Journal of Personality and Social Psychology,* 1970, **15**, 283-293.

Sensenig, J., & Brehm, J. W. Attitude change from an implied threat to attitudinal freedom. *Journal of Personality and Social Psychology,* 1968, **8**, 324-330.

Shaffer, D. R., & Hendrick, C. Effects of actual effort and anticipated effort on task enhancement. *Journal of Experimental Social Psychology,* 1971, **7**, 435-447.

Sherman, S. J. Attitudinal effects of unforeseen consequences. *Journal of Personality and Social Psychology,* 1970, **16**, 510-520.

Skinner, B. F. *Beyond freedom and dignity.* New York: Knopf, 1971.

Steiner, I. D. Perceived freedom. In L. Berkowitz (Ed.), *Advances in experimental social psychology.* Vol. 5. New York: Academic Press, 1970.

Walster, E., & Festinger, L. The effectiveness of "overheard" persuasive communications. *Journal of Abnormal and Social Psychology,* 1962, **65**, 395-402.

Weiner, Judith A. Psychological reactance from involuntary restriction of choice alternatives. Unpublished manuscript, Duke University, 1963.

Wicklund, R. A. Regret as a result of threat to decision freedom. Unpublished doctoral dissertation, Duke University, 1968.

Wicklund, R. A. Prechoice preference reversal as a result of threat to decision freedom. *Journal of Personality and Social Psychology,* 1970, **14**, 8-17.

Wicklund, R. A., & Brehm, J. W. Effects of censorship on attitude change and desire to hear a communication. Unpublished manuscript, Duke University, 1967.

Wicklund, R. A., & Brehm, J. W. Attitude change as a function of felt competence and threat to attitudinal freedom. *Journal of Experimental Social Psychology,* 1968, **4**, 64-75.

Wicklund, R. A., Cooper, J., & Linder, D. E. Effects of expected effort on attitude change prior to exposure. *Journal of Experimental Social Psychology,* 1967, **3**, 416-428.

Wicklund, R. A., Slattum, V., & Solomon, E. Effects of implied pressure toward commitment on ratings of choice alternatives. *Journal of Experimental Social Psychology,* 1970, **6**, 449-457.

Worchel, S. The effect of simple frustration, violated expectancy, and reactance on the instigation to aggression. Unpublished doctoral dissertation, Duke University, 1971.

Worchel, S., & Arnold, S. E. The effects of censorship and attractiveness of the censor on attitude change. *Journal of Experimental Social Psychology*, 1973, **9**, 365-377.

Worchel, S., & Brehm, J. W. Effect of threats to attitudinal freedom as a function of agreement with the communicator. *Journal of Personality and Social Psychology*, 1970, **14**, 18-22.

Worchel, S., & Brehm, J. W. Direct and implied social restoration of freedom. *Journal of Personality and Social Psychology*, 1971, **18**, 294-304.

Wright, H. F. *The influence of barriers upon strength of motivation.* Durham, N.C.: Duke University Press, 1937.

Zander, A. F. A study of experimental frustration. *Psychological Monographs*, 1944, **56** (Whole No. 256), 1-38.

Zimbrado, P.G. The effect of effort and improvisation on self-persuasion produced by role-playing. *Journal of Experimental Social Psychology*, 1965, **1**, 103-120.

Zimbardo, P. G. The human choice: Individuation, reason, and order versus deindividuation, impulse, and chaos. In W. J. Arnold & D. Levine (Eds.), *Nebraska symposium on motivation*. Vol. 17. Lincoln, Neb.: University of Nebraska Press, 1969.

FREEDOM AND REACTANCE

INDEXES

AUTHOR INDEX

Numbers in *italics* refer to the pages on which the complete references are listed.

SUBJECT INDEX

A

Achievement orientation, 95-97, 121, 125-128, 134
Aggression, 139-148
Attractiveness of alternatives, 128-130, 163-165, 168
Avoidance of freedom, 184-186
Awareness of options, 40-41, 43-45, 117-119, 162

B

Balance theory, 4-5, 15, 21, 33-34, 71

C

Censorship, 30-35
Choice certainty, 10, 155-156, 175-176
Cognitive dissonance, 16, 93, 97-100, 104-106, 109, 115-116, 121-122, 130-133, 151, 156-158, 162, 167, 169-172

O

One-sided communication, 44-45
Outcome freedom, 180

P

Personal space, 85-89
Predecisional convergence, 9, 150, 159-162, 165-168
Pressure theory, 94-95, 100, 121, 134
Prior demonstration of freedom, 55-61

R

Reactance suppression, 81-85
Regret, 169-172

S

Secondary reinforcement, 102
Selective attention, 108
Selective exposure, 176
Simultaneous threats, 22-24, 85-90
Size estimation, 108
Skill vs. chance, 116-117
Social equity, 16-17
Social responsibility norm, 35
Sour grapes, 101

V

Validation of barriers, 92-93, 120